CONTENTS

INTRODUCTION

Scouting isn't a science, it's an imperfect, ever-evolving art. And while team-building philosophies will differ from team to team, the common denominator is that the NFL Draft is the best way to construct a championship roster.

This 2016 draft class contains several players who will go on to make Pro Bowls, win Super Bowls, and maybe even reach the Hall of Fame. Who are those impact players? What makes them so special? Where is their best fit? This draft preview will help answer those questions.

The reports created for this guide were formed through film study, in-person scouting, and a number of other variables, including various metrics, interviews, and information from around the league. In a nutshell, the scouting process is a jigsaw puzzle. There are countless puzzle pieces for each prospect, and the goal is to connect as many of those pieces together to create a clearer picture of who that player will be in the NFL.

At the top of this year's class, there are several blue-chip prospects who have an argument to be the best player overall in the draft. Ole Miss left tackle Laremy Tunsil was born to play the position in the NFL, with his rare body control and movement skills. UCLA linebacker Myles Jack would be one of the first running backs drafted if he wanted to focus on offense, but instead he will be one of the first defensive players off the board due to his versatile and rangy athleticism. Florida State defensive back Jalen Ramsey will be a safety for some teams and a cornerback for others, but the best label to describe his abilities might simply be "playmaker." Ohio State defensive end Joey Bosa has the physical gifts and natural instincts to threaten the pocket in a number of different ways, using his power, burst, and technique in unison. Buckeyes running back Ezekiel Elliott might not be on the Todd Gurley level, but he is a difference-maker worthy of early first-round consideration because he is above average in almost every area needed to be a highly productive pro running back.

And that's just the top five. This guide takes an in-depth look at 60 of the best prospects that this draft class has to offer, connecting the puzzle pieces to best portray their strengths and weaknesses as football players.

ACKNOWLEDGMENTS

Beauty is in the eye of the beholder. That sentiment is true in many aspects of life and especially in scouting. No two sets of eyes see the same thing, which is why even the most respected football minds will have such varied opinions on prospects in the NFL Draft. Perspective is a powerful tool.

Will the draft play out exactly in this order, 1 through 60? Of course not, but that wasn't my goal when putting this guide together. My goal was to poll several scouts around the league and narrow down 60 of the best players in this draft based on that feedback, providing analyses and evaluations to paint the picture of each prospect. Updated character or injury information (i.e., Notre Dame linebacker Jaylon Smith's injured knee) might change some grades in the eight weeks between when this guide went to print in early March and the 2016 NFL Draft on April 28.

Countless people contributed to this book, including friends, coaches, and mentors from around the NFL and scouting world, who continue to teach me every day. I'm grateful for their experienced knowledge, considerate advice, and willingness to share insight or simply talk shop. This guide to the top prospects in the 2016 NFL Draft is dedicated to legendary longtime NFL scout C.O. Brocato, who taught me the basics. He will never be forgotten and belongs in the Pro Football Hall of Fame.

The team at Triumph Books was instrumental in coordinating and executing the vision of this project. Not to be forgotten is the Sports Xchange family and everyone at NFLDraftScout.com, the best source of independent scouting information in the industry. And most importantly, my family and main inspirations, including my wife, Stephanie, and six-month-old son, Kegan. I'm blessed to have such an understanding and loving support system, allowing me to eat, drink, and breathe football and not work a day in my life.

NFL DRAFT

ELITE 60

LAREMY TUNSIL
OT / OLE MISS

Name: Laremy Tunsil

Ht: 6'7"   **Wt:** 310

Hometown/High School: Lake City, FL / Columbia

Class: Junior

Number: 78

DOB: August 2, 1994

Career Highlights: Second-Team All-SEC (2014), Freshman All-SEC (2013)

Did You Know? Never made First-Team All-SEC or earned SEC Offensive Lineman of the Week honors over his three-year Ole Miss career, mainly because he didn't play a full season in college.

Fun Fact: Credits facing high school teammate Timmy Jernigan (Baltimore Ravens second-round pick in 2014 out of Florida State) in practice every day for his development into a five-star recruit.

Ideal Team Fit: Due to his natural balance, athleticism, and movement skills, Tunsil has a very high ceiling and should step into a starting left tackle role as a rookie, making him a strong candidate for the Tennessee Titans with the No. 1 overall pick.

NFL Comparison: Trent Williams

The most talented NFL prospect in his class, Laremy Tunsil was also the top-ranked offensive lineman as a high school recruit, committing to Ole Miss over Alabama and Georgia. He worked his way into the starting lineup in the third game of 2013 and started nine games as a true freshman, earning Freshman All-SEC honors. He started 11 games at left tackle in 2014 as a sophomore (missed two due to injury), earning second-team All-SEC honors. Tunsil served a seven-game NCAA suspension to begin the 2015 season, starting the final six games at left tackle for the Rebels.

STRENGTHS: Moldable frame with long arms. Finely tuned athlete with tremendous balance and change of direction to appear effortless in pass-sets. Light feet and flexible joints in his kick-slide to handle speed, coming to balance on the move and staying square to rushers. Sinks and anchors to strengthen his core, withstand rip moves, and hold his ground at the point of attack. Peppers defenders with strong hands, quick punch, and rapid recoil to load up and strike again—keeps his elbows inside for an accurate strike zone. Coordinated feet with blocking range to routinely eliminate defenders at the second level and on the perimeter, sealing linebackers and staying on his feet. Physical mind-set and always looking for someone to block. Smart and quickly picks up defenders on delayed blitzes and combo blocks.

WEAKNESSES: Room to add more bulk and get stronger. Shows the core power needed when he can sink and square, but not as stout with defenders off his edge. Overeager at times and needs to stay patient to not get ahead of the play design. Needs to eliminate the false-start penalties and stay focused through the whistle. Doesn't always play as mean as his intentions. Arrested (June 2015) following a domestic dispute with his stepfather (charges eventually dropped), which led to NCAA investigations and a seven-game suspension for accepting impermissible benefits. Routinely banged up over his career, including a fractured right fibula and dislocated ankle in the 2014 bowl game, which required surgery and sidelined him for 2015 spring drills.

SUMMARY: A three-year starter at left tackle, Tunsil was a much ballyhooed recruit and immediately lived up to the hype at Ole Miss, allowing only one sack as a true freshman starter in the SEC. He's a nimble big man with a rare athletic skill-set for the position, showing above-average balance and flexibility to easily bend, handle speed, and absorb power at the point of attack. He missed some time the past two seasons due to injuries and other issues, which should be vetted. He's not a perfect player, but his flaws are more nit-picking than true weaknesses, and potential injuries are the only obstacles keeping Tunsil from being one of the better left tackles at the next level.

CAREER STATS

SEASON	GP/GS	POS
2013	12/9	LT
2014	11/11	LT
2015	6/6	LT
Career	29/26	LT

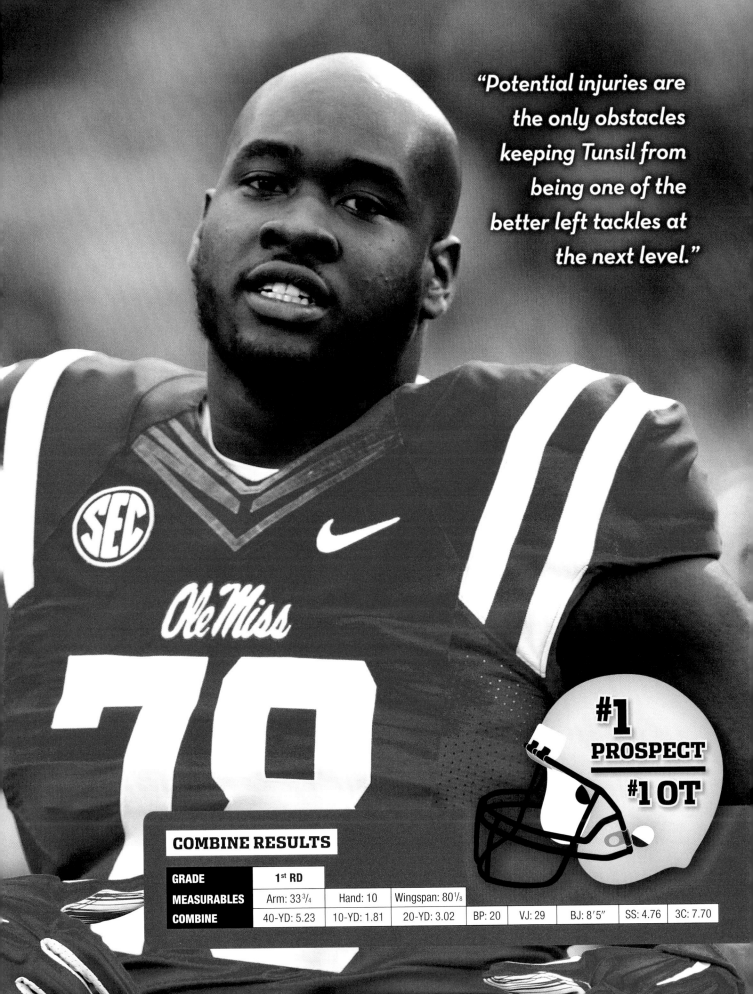

"Potential injuries are the only obstacles keeping Tunsil from being one of the better left tackles at the next level."

#1 PROSPECT
#1 OT

COMBINE RESULTS

GRADE	1ˢᵗ RD							
MEASURABLES	Arm: 33¾	Hand: 10	Wingspan: 80⅛					
COMBINE	40-YD: 5.23	10-YD: 1.81	20-YD: 3.02	BP: 20	VJ: 29	BJ: 8'5"	SS: 4.76	3C: 7.70

MYLES JACK
LB / UCLA

Name: Myles Jack

Ht: 6'1" **Wt:** 245

Hometown/High School: Bellevue, WA / Bellevue

Class: Junior

Number: 30

DOB: September 3, 1995

Career Highlights: Second-Team All-Pac-12 (2014), Freshman All-American (2013), Offensive and Defensive Pac-12 Freshman of the Year (2013), Second-Team All-Pac-12 (2013)

Did You Know? A do-it-all playmaker, Jack averaged 5.7 yards per carry as a running back during his time at UCLA, with 11 offensive touchdowns, and he also blocked a kick on special teams.

Fun Fact: Following his knee injury last fall, Jack made the bold decision to withdraw from school mid-season in order to focus on his rehab and prepare for the NFL Draft.

Ideal Team Fit: With his rare athleticism for the position, Jack fits best as a weak-side linebacker in a 4-3 scheme, but his versatile skill-set extends to any linebacker spot, and smart defensive coordinators will adjust the personnel to accommodate his vast talent.

NFL Comparison: NaVorro Bowman

One of the most versatile players in the country, Myles Jack saw the field early in his collegiate career as a two-way true freshman for UCLA, recording 75 tackles on defense and seven TDs on offense. Jack started all 13 games in 2014 as a sophomore, finishing second on the team with 88 tackles to earn second-team All-Pac-12 honors for the second straight year. His junior season was cut short after three games due to a knee injury, but Jack elected to leave school early for the 2016 NFL Draft.

STRENGTHS: Explosive athlete with rare movement skills and contact balance for the position. Swivel hips, balanced body control, and rubber joints to smoothly change directions. Chase speed to track down players from behind. Physical and not shy about stacking the edge and taking on blocks at the line of scrimmage. Arrives with violent intentions as a tackler, finishing with pop. Consistent reads to diagnose quickly and put himself in position to make plays. Comfortable in space with above-average coverage skills for the position, playing sticky coverage and collecting himself well in his pedal/transition to redirect on the move. Excellent ball skills and reflexes at the catch point (23 passes defended and four interceptions in 28 starts). Passionate self-starter and brings the same intensity on every play. Impressive determination to return from his knee injury and compete at the NFL Combine.

WEAKNESSES: Average-at-best size and length, lacking the frame to get much bigger. Can be eaten up by blockers near the offensive line and needs to improve his stack-shed technique to better disengage. Lacks the long arms to easily keep himself clean. Room to clean up his technique and pad level as a tackler, lowering his strike zone. A more disciplined approach at the contact point will also help him avoid horse-collar and other penalties. Can be fooled by play-action and misdirection, causing him to be late in coverage. Limited experience as a blitzer. Suffered a serious knee injury that required surgery (September 2015), tearing the anterior meniscus in his right knee.

SUMMARY: A three-year starter, Jack was a two-way player in college at running back and linebacker, but lined up primarily as a hybrid linebacker/safety at UCLA who was asked to cover over the slot and in space. He is an athletic specimen with elite pursuit speed and an above-average mental processor to know everything going on around him. Jack doesn't have ideal size or power for the position and needs to become more of a technician, but he doesn't back down at the point of attack and brings the same attitude each snap. He is at his best in space with exceptional cover skills due to his loose athleticism, easy change of direction, and ball skills, entering the NFL as the best cover linebacker prospect since Luke Kuechly.

CAREER STATS

SEASON	GP/GS	TACKLES	TFL	SACKS	FF	INT
2013	13/12	75	7.0	1.0	0	2
2014	13/13	88	8.0	0.0	0	1
2015	3/3	15	0.0	0.0	0	1
Career	29/28	178	15.0	1.0	0	4

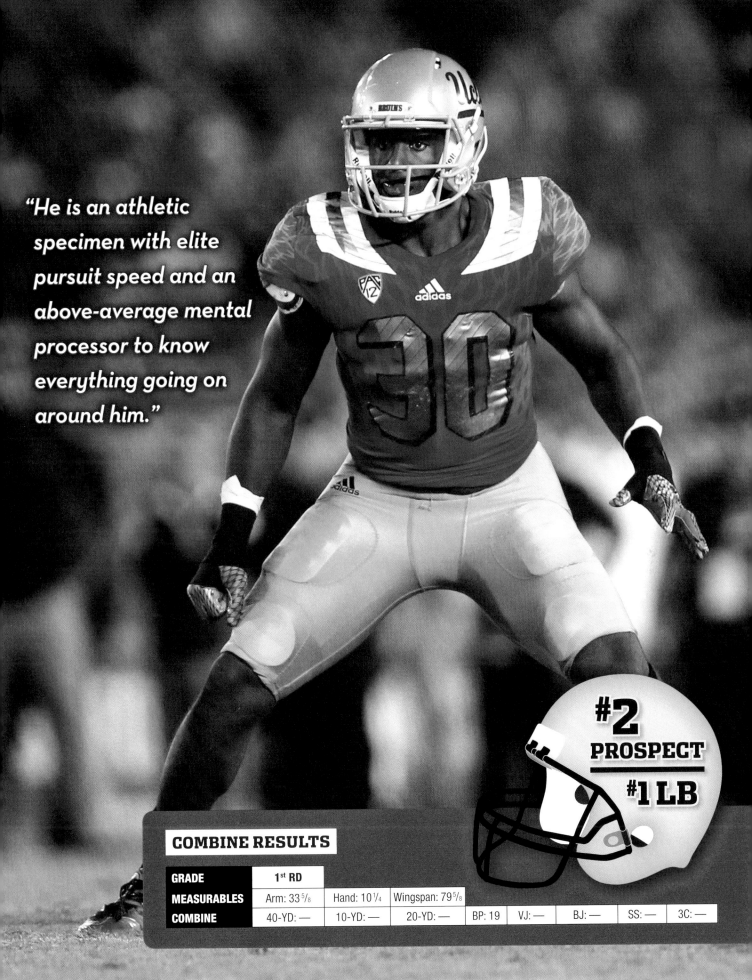

"He is an athletic specimen with elite pursuit speed and an above-average mental processor to know everything going on around him."

#2 PROSPECT
#1 LB

COMBINE RESULTS

GRADE	1st RD							
MEASURABLES	Arm: 33 5/8	Hand: 10 1/4	Wingspan: 79 5/8					
COMBINE	40-YD: —	10-YD: —	20-YD: —	BP: 19	VJ: —	BJ: —	SS: —	3C: —

JALEN RAMSEY
S / FLORIDA STATE

Name: Jalen Ramsey

Ht: 6′1¼″ **Wt:** 209

Hometown/High School: Smyrna, TN / Brentwood Academy

Class: Junior

Number: 8

DOB: October 24, 1994

Career Highlights: Consensus All-American (2015), First-Team All-ACC (2015), All-American (2014), First-Team All-ACC (2014), Freshman All-American (2013), BCS National Champion (2013)

Did You Know? Won both the ACC indoor and outdoor long-jump titles in 2015 and ran the leadoff leg of Florida State's ACC champion 4x100 relay team.

Fun Fact: Due to double numbers when playing special teams, Ramsey was given permission by Heisman-winning Seminoles quarterback Charlie Ward to wear his retired No. 17 when needed.

Ideal Team Fit: While he can play cornerback and some teams will look to keep him on the outside, Ramsey is at his best in a nickel safety role where he can be an explosive playmaker.

NFL Comparison: Tyrann Mathieu

Jalen Ramsey was one of the best players on the Florida State roster the moment he arrived in Tallahassee, splitting his playing time all over the secondary for the Seminoles. He started his true freshman season at cornerback before moving to free safety due to injury, recording 49 tackles, two passes defended, and an interception. Ramsey started all 14 games at the "STAR" (hybrid nickel back) position as a sophomore and led the team with 14 passes defended, earning All-America and All-ACC honors. He moved to boundary cornerback as a junior in 2015, and although he didn't record an interception, Ramsey led the Seminoles in passes defended (10) for the second straight season and earned consensus All-America honors.

STRENGTHS: Tall, long-armed athlete with adequate muscle tone. Long-striding with terrific range, acceleration, and closing speed. Light feet and lateral agility to mirror or stay in phase with receivers down the field. Fluid change-of-direction skills, collecting himself with the natural flexibility to break down on the move. Drops his hips and goes from 0-to-60 quickly. NFL-level eyes, vision, and spatial awareness, seeing the field well with patience and anticipation. Uses his length exceptionally to press, get his hands on the ball, wrap tackle, and shed blocks. Effective dip and bend as an edge blitzer. Extensive special teams experience as a gunner, playing on both kickoff and punt coverages. Playmaker with the ball, averaging 23.4 yards per return on turnovers. Locked-in competitor with a fearless alpha-male personality and yearning to be great. Didn't miss a start at FSU and offers versatility with starting experience at safety, cornerback, and hybrid versions of both.

WEAKNESSES: Room to add bulk and needs to develop his functional strength to better disengage blocks. Room to clean up his tackling technique, patience, and pad level. Will get run over in the NFL if he doesn't use better lower-body bend. Loves to bait throws, but will allow his eyes to pay rent in the backfield, giving up completions. Upright backpedal and lacks easy transitional movements due to his leggy athleticism. Inconsistent ball skills and needs to be a better finisher at the catch point, dropping several INTs on film.

SUMMARY: A three-year starter, Ramsey gained experience in zone, press, and off-man coverage. His 2014 game film as a hybrid safety was better than his 2015 game film at boundary cornerback, but he can do everything you want in the secondary. If you combined a safety, cornerback, and linebacker into one prospect, the result would look something like Ramsey, who is blessed with inherent instincts and intuition along with the size and athletic profile to be a difference maker. It's rare to see defensive backs mentioned as worthy of the No. 1 overall selection in the NFL Draft, but Ramsey deserves it.

CAREER STATS

SEASON	GP/GS	TACKLES	TFL	SACKS	FF	PASS DEF	INT
2013	14/14	49	2.0	1.0	1	2	1
2014	14/14	79	9.5	3.0	2	14	2
2015	12/12	52	4.0	1.0	0	10	0
Career	40/40	180	15.5	5.0	3	26	3

"If you combined a safety, cornerback, and linebacker into one prospect, the result would look something like Ramsey."

#3 PROSPECT
#1 S

COMBINE RESULTS

GRADE	1st RD							
MEASURABLES	Arm: 33 3/8	Hand: 9 1/2	Wingspan: 79 5/8					
COMBINE	40-YD: 4.41	10-YD: 1.51	20-YD: 2.57	BP: 14	VJ: 41 1/2	BJ: 11'3"	SS: 4.18	3C: 6.94

JOEY BOSA
DE / OHIO STATE

Name: Joey Bosa

Ht: 6′5¼″ **Wt:** 269

Hometown/High School: Fort Lauderdale, FL / St. Thomas Aquinas

Class: Junior

Number: 97

DOB: July 11, 1995

Career Highlights: Smith-Brown Big Ten Defensive Lineman of the Year (2015), First-Team All–Big Ten (2015), CFP National Champion (2015), Nagurski-Woodson Big Ten Defensive Player of the Year (2014), Unanimous All-American (2014), First-Team All–Big Ten (2014), Freshman All-American (2013), Honorable Mention All–Big Ten (2013)

Did You Know? If Bosa is drafted in the first round, he will join an exclusive group of fathers-and-sons who were both selected in the NFL Draft's opening round (John Bosa was a first-rounder in 1987).

Fun Fact: Although he jumped to the NFL early, Ohio State won't be Bosa-less as his younger brother and five-star recruit, Nick Bosa, arrives in Columbus this spring.

Ideal Team Fit: With his well-rounded skill-set versus the pass and the run, Bosa is best suited as a left defensive end in a four-man front like the Dallas Cowboys, but he is scheme-versatile to fit even and odd fronts.

NFL Comparison: Chris Long

A prospect worthy of the No. 1 overall pick, Joey Bosa made an instant impact as a true freshman in Columbus and had his best season as a sophomore and core member of the Buckeyes' national title team. A unanimous All-American, Bosa tallied 21 tackles for loss and 13.5 sacks, taking home the Big Ten's Defensive Player of the Year award. Although his production took a dip in 2015, Bosa was just as disruptive, earning First-Team All–Big Ten honors for the second straight year.

STRENGTHS: Grown-man strength with an NFL build and body strength. Balanced athlete with natural bend, flexibility, and initial quickness. Controls his momentum and easily converts his first step to power, sinking and rushing with low pad level to put blockers on skates. Athletic repertoire of rush moves with an innate understanding of how to use his hands and length to set up moves. Comfortable on his feet to drop and play in space. Excellent secondary quickness and doesn't take himself out of plays, due to his hustle and ball awareness. Stacks and leverages blocks to stay home, hold contain, and force the action inside. Natural core power and knows how to use it, rarely playing on his heels. Very good break-down skills to reset his eyes, collect himself, and finish. Violent striker and doesn't miss tackles when he's in the area. Plays with a high degree of toughness and is accustomed to facing double- and triple-teams. Productive résumé with 50.5 tackles for loss and 26 sacks over his 37 career starts.

WEAKNESSES: Not a quick-twitch rusher or elite explosion athlete. Still developing his body mechanics as an edge rusher and needs to improve his inside shoulder dip. Too reactionary at times with room to improve his anticipation. Will occasionally misread option and zone plays and needs to maintain his gap and outside responsibilities. Snap discipline needs tweaking (five offside penalties in a two-game stretch in 2015). Suspended for the 2015 season opener due to a violation of team rules.

SUMMARY: A three-year starter, Bosa lined up in a three-point stance, mostly at left defensive end, but also on the right side and sometimes inside as a three-technique or standing up as a spying linebacker. He is very physically gifted, but even better, he knows how to use those gifts and works his tail off to maximize his potential. Bosa displays the instincts, preparation, and understanding of leverage that allow him to be successful, setting up his moves, creating separation from blockers and seeing through bodies—Ohio State defensive coordinator Luke Fickell probably said it best, "There's nothing he can't do." Although he might not be a consistent double-digit sack artist in the NFL, Bosa is a scheme-versatile player with the dominant traits to consistently impact the game versus the pass and the run at the next level.

CAREER STATS

SEASON	GP/GS	TACKLES	TFL	SACKS	FF	INT
2013	14/10	44	13.5	7.5	0	0
2014	12/12	55	21.0	13.5	4	0
2015	15/15	51	16.0	5.0	1	1
Career	41/37	150	50.5	26.0	5	1

"Bosa is very physically gifted, but even better, he knows how to use those gifts and works his tail off to maximize his potential."

#4 PROSPECT
#1 DE

COMBINE RESULTS

GRADE	1st RD							
MEASURABLES	Arm: 33⅜	Hand: 10¼	Wingspan: 79¾					
COMBINE	40-YD: 4.86	10-YD: 1.68	20-YD: 2.83	BP: 24	VJ: 32	BJ: 10'0"	SS: 4.21	3C: 6.89

EZEKIEL ELLIOTT
RB / OHIO STATE

Name: Ezekiel Elliott

Ht: 5'11¾" **Wt:** 225

Hometown/High School: St. Louis, MO / John Burroughs

Class: Junior

Number: 15

DOB: July 22, 1995

Career Highlights: Graham-George Big Ten Offensive Player of the Year (2015), Ameche-Dayne Big Ten Running back of the Year (2015), First-Team All–Big Ten (2015), CFP National Champion (2015), CFP National Championship Game Offensive MVP (2015), Sugar Bowl Offensive MVP (2015), James E. Sullivan Award (2015)

Did You Know? Won four state championships in track & field at the Missouri Class 3 state championships in the 100- and 200-meter dash, 110-meter high hurdles, and 300-meter hurdles.

Fun Fact: Coached in high school by Gus Frerotte, former Tulsa star and NFL QB

Ideal Team Fit: Best suited for a gap-run scheme, but Elliott has the well-rounded skill-set to fit any blocking scheme or run style. He is the type of player that all 32 teams will have on the draft board.

NFL Comparison: Frank Gore

Ezekiel Elliott gained legendary status in the state of Ohio with his performance down the stretch in 2014, recording back-to-back-to-back 200-yard rushing performances in the Big Ten Championship Game (220 yards vs. Wisconsin), Sugar Bowl (230 yards vs. Alabama), and National Championship Game (246 yards vs. Oregon). He entered his junior season in 2015 as the Heisman front-runner and, although he didn't win the award, his rushing totals from 2014 (1,878) and 2015 (1,821) rank second and third on Ohio State's all-time single-season list. Elliott leaves Ohio State after his junior season as the No. 2 rusher (3,961 yards) in program history, just behind two-time Heisman winner Archie Griffin.

STRENGTHS: Extremely well-rounded as a runner with ideal size for the position along with coordinated footwork and outstanding vision to quickly read his blocks and react. Does an excellent job marrying his eyes with his feet to read, cut, and go in fluid motion, transitioning his weight flawlessly in his movements. Runs with natural pad level and fantastic forward lean, using his balance, leg drive, and relentless fight to move the chains and finish with authority. Shines at the second level, gaining speed in the open field to separate from pursuing defenders and stretch out his stride. Quick, strong hands as a pass-catcher to pluck away from his body (58 career receptions) and will always be a threat to create after the catch. Does some of his best work away from the ball, throwing his body around as a blocker. Praised by his coaches for his intelligence, leadership, and understanding of situational football. Proven workhorse with the ability to put the offense on his shoulders while staying fresh late in games.

WEAKNESSES: Slow to get past the line of scrimmage at times due to his patience, giving his blockers too much time and allowing defenders to react. Stubbornly follows the design of the run—as he's coached to do—but needs to be a better freelancer if the opportunity presents itself. Elliott isn't known as a "me" player, but he had an immature moment following the Michigan State loss in 2015, publicly criticizing the play-calling and Ohio State coaches.

SUMMARY: The top-rated running back prospect in the 2016 class, "Zeke" Elliott needs refinement in a few areas, but it's tough to find glaring weaknesses in his run style, which is why NFL teams have stamped him with a first-round grade. He has exceptional balance and center of gravity to pick up yards after contact with the vision and acceleration to be a home-run finisher any time he touches the ball. Elliott projects as a starting running back in the NFL capable of high-volume touches and is ideally suited in the gap-run game, but fits every offensive scheme due to his versatility.

CAREER STATS

SEASON	GP/GS	RUSH ATT	RUSH YD	RUSH AVG	RUSH TD	REC	REC YD	REC AVG	REC TD
2013	11/0	30	262	8.7	2	3	23	7.7	1
2014	15/14	273	1,878	6.9	18	28	220	7.9	0
2015	13/13	289	1,821	6.3	23	27	206	7.6	0
Career	39/27	592	3,961	6.7	43	58	449	7.7	1

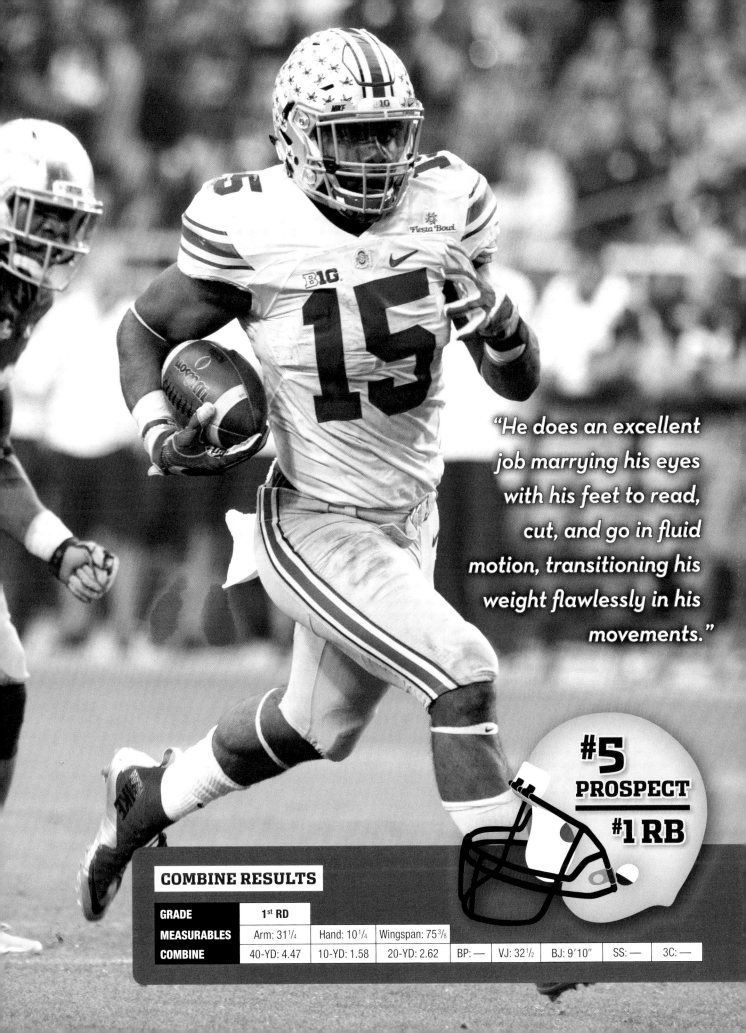

"He does an excellent job marrying his eyes with his feet to read, cut, and go in fluid motion, transitioning his weight flawlessly in his movements."

#5 PROSPECT

#1 RB

COMBINE RESULTS

GRADE	1st RD							
MEASURABLES	Arm: 31¼	Hand: 10¼	Wingspan: 75⅜					
COMBINE	40-YD: 4.47	10-YD: 1.58	20-YD: 2.62	BP: —	VJ: 32½	BJ: 9'10"	SS: —	3C: —

LAQUON TREADWELL
WR / OLE MISS

Name: Laquon Treadwell

Ht: 6′2″ **Wt:** 221

Hometown/High School: Crete, IL / Crete-Monee

Class: Junior

Number: 1

DOB: June 14, 1995

Career Highlights: All-American (2015), First-Team All-SEC (2015), Biletnikoff Award Finalist (2015), SEC Freshman of the Year (2013)

Did You Know? Leaves Ole Miss with the school record for career receptions (202) and is the first SEC player to record 100-plus receiving yards and at least one touchdown in five straight games.

Fun Fact: Brings an added wrinkle to the offense due to his arm talent to be a threat as a passer, completing all three of his pass attempts in 2015 for 134 yards and a touchdown.

Ideal Team Fit: With experience inside and outside, Treadwell can line up anywhere on offense, but his best fit is for a team in the market for an "X" receiver, like the Cleveland Browns or San Francisco 49ers.

NFL Comparison: A less dynamic Dez Bryant

The SEC has produced many premier wide-receiver prospects in recent memory, like Amari Cooper, Mike Evans, Odell Beckham Jr., A.J. Green, and Julio Jones. Laquon Treadwell will soon add his name to that list as one of the top-10 talents available in the 2016 draft class. A three-year starter, Treadwell lined up everywhere in the Ole Miss offense and was consistently productive despite defenses game-planning against him. In 2014 he suffered a gruesome left leg injury (broken fibula, dislocated ankle), but he returned stronger as a junior in 2015, leading the SEC in catches (82), receiving yards (1,153), and TD receptions (11).

STRENGTHS: Well-built for the position with a muscular upper body and sleek definition. Long arms and large hands to create a sizeable catching radius. Natural plucker with vacuum hands away from his body, snatching anything in his general direction. Outstanding on 50-50 balls, showing above-average body control and hand-eye coordination. Lacks sprinter speed, but is faster than expected due to strong, decisive strides. Shows the ability to push routes, sink, and quickly locate the football. Plays with grown-man strength to brush off tackle attempts and get every yard possible—rarely phased by initial tackler in college due to his balance and power. Run-after-catch ability with his strength and athleticism, stretching screens into big gains. Takes pride in his blocking. Strong-minded competitor and wired right for professional football. Grounded, mature personality for his age and handled adversity well after his 2014 season-ending injury.

WEAKNESSES: Route running is still a work-in-progress and wasn't asked to run a full tree in the Ole Miss offense. Needs to rely more on his footwork at the top of routes to create separation. Speed is average for the position, lacking a second gear vertically to easily gain a step. Has the occasional focus drop, running before securing the catch. His physicality is his calling card, but will also lead to offensive interference penalties with the way he uses his hands. Emotionally charged competitor, which led to several false start and unsportsmanlike penalties at Ole Miss.

SUMMARY: Treadwell lined up inside and outside at Ole Miss and was consistently productive despite defenses keying on him, leading the SEC in receiving in 2015. He has exceptional ball skills and catching radius with strong hands to pluck above his head or scoop off his shoelaces—if the throw is anywhere within a few feet of his body, he'll attack it. Although soft-spoken, Treadwell is highly respected and plays like a warrior. He isn't a sudden athlete, but Treadwell plays with athletic twitch and power to be a threat after the catch, with the skill-set to become a legitimate No. 1 target in the NFL.

CAREER STATS

SEASON	GP/GS	REC	REC YD	REC AVG	REC TD
2013	13/13	72	608	8.4	5
2014	8/8	48	632	13.2	5
2015	13/13	82	1,153	14.1	11
Career	34/34	202	2,393	11.8	21

"Treadwell has exceptional ball skills and catching radius with strong hands to pluck above his head or scoop off his shoelaces."

#6 PROSPECT
#1 WR

COMBINE RESULTS

GRADE	1ST RD							
MEASURABLES	Arm: 33³/₈	Hand: 9½	Wingspan: 80½					
COMBINE	40-YD: —	10-YD: —	20-YD: —	BP: 12	VJ: 33	BJ: 9'9"	SS: —	3C: —

DEFOREST BUCKNER
DE / OREGON

Name: DeForest Buckner

Ht: 6'7" **Wt:** 291

Hometown/High School: Waianae, HI / Punahou

Class: Senior

Number: 44

DOB: March 17, 1992

Career Highlights: Oregon Defensive MVP (2015), Pat Tillman Pac-12 Defensive Player of the Year (2015), First-Team All-Pac-12 (2015), Pac-12 Morris Trophy (2015), Second-Team All-Pac-12 (2014)

Did You Know? Left his mark in the Pac-12 as opposing offensive linemen voted him as the winner of the Pac-12's Morris Trophy, and Stanford's David Shaw described Buckner by saying, "If you're building a defensive lineman, that's what you build."

Fun Fact: Only the second Oregon Duck to earn Pac-12's top defensive player award, joining former first-round pick Haloti Ngata, who won the award in 2005.

Ideal Team Fit: Similar to his role at Oregon, Buckner's best fit is in a 3-4 base as a five-technique defensive end for a team like the Chicago Bears, but he has the scheme-diverse skill-set to also fit inside or outside for four-man fronts.

NFL Comparison: Calais Campbell

The Hawaii-to-Oregon recruiting pipeline produced the No. 2 overall selection in the 2015 NFL Draft (Marcus Mariota) and might produce another top-10 pick this year. DeForest Buckner was part of a rotation his first two years in Eugene before becoming a full-time starter as a junior, leading Oregon with 13 tackles for loss. He passed on the NFL to return for his senior season and had his most productive season, recording a team-best 17 tackles for loss and 10.5 sacks to earn numerous awards and accolades.

STRENGTHS: Looks the part with a tall, long frame and growth potential to add bulk. Has a massive wingspan and uses his length to unglue himself from blocks or create spacing at the point of attack, locking out, setting the edge, and preventing angle blocks. Quickly stacks and sheds, using pop in his hands to work off contact. Fluid lower body and athletic footwork. Plays low for a man his size with good bend, making it tough for blockers to attack his chest. Chase skills and hustle to catch ball carriers in pursuit. Uses his upper body and initial momentum to generate push off the snap. Rarely met by single blocks, attracting double-teams or chips. Uses his length to swallow ball carriers as a tackler and obstruct passing lanes (10 career passes defended). Quiet, reserved personality off the field, but warrior-mentality on the field, giving full-go whenever he steps between the lines. Versatile experience, lining up inside and outside in Oregon's multiple fronts—also saw action on special teams coverages.

WEAKNESSES: Leverage can be an issue due to his height. Struggles to recoil and reset himself after his initial move stalls. Still learning how to set up his pass rush sequence and counter moves. Only average snap anticipation. Needs to know his limitations as a pass rusher and not sacrifice the edge. Still learning how to use his hands and consistently convert speed to power—more of a reactor as a pass rusher. Inconsistent tackler on the move, losing balance in space. Needs to show more of a killer instinct on each snap.

SUMMARY: A three-year starter, Buckner played primarily as a defensive end in Oregon's 3-4 base, lining up as the four-, five-, or six-technique, but also saw snaps inside in the A-gap or at nose tackle. He plays with explosive movements and terrific body control for his size, flashing heavy hands and initial power to be a disruptive force, although he's still learning how to use his hands and string together rush moves. Buckner showed steady improvement at Oregon and should get even better with NFL coaching, projecting better than his former teammate Arik Armstead (17th overall pick to the 49ers in the 2015 NFL Draft).

CAREER STATS

SEASON	GP/GS	TACKLES	TFL	SACKS	FF
2012	13/2	29	2.5	1.0	0
2013	13/8	39	3.5	2.5	1
2014	15/15	81	13.0	4.0	1
2015	13/13	83	17.0	10.5	0
Career	54/38	232	36.0	17.0	2

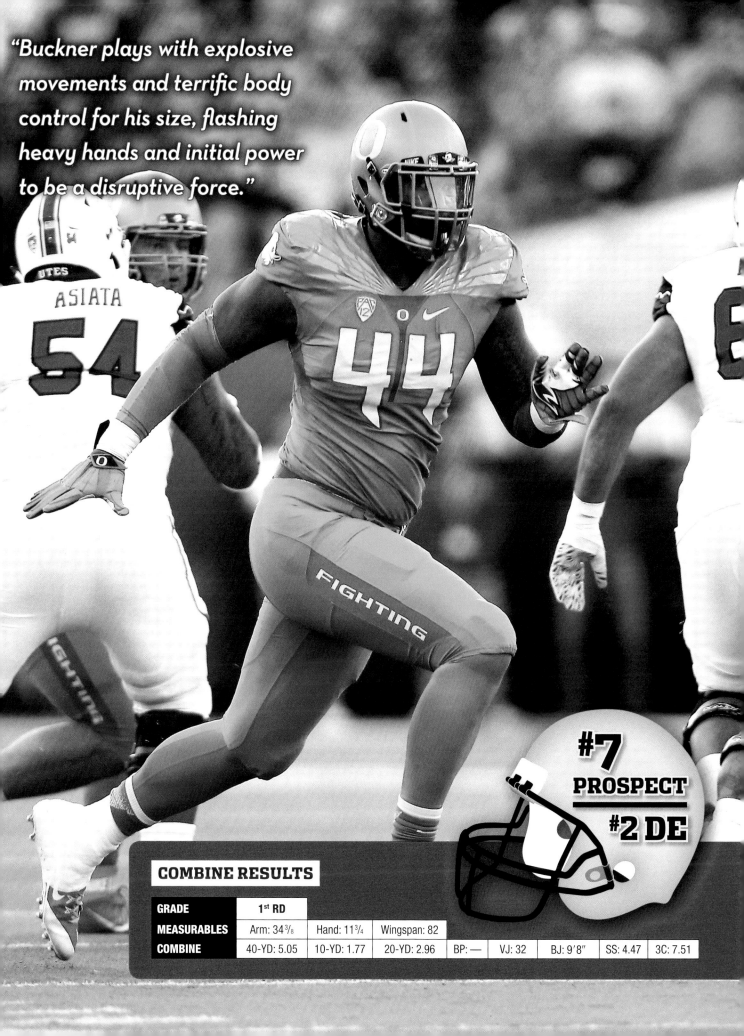

"Buckner plays with explosive movements and terrific body control for his size, flashing heavy hands and initial power to be a disruptive force."

#7 PROSPECT

#2 DE

COMBINE RESULTS

GRADE	1ˢᵗ RD							
MEASURABLES	Arm: 34³⁄₈	Hand: 11³⁄₄	Wingspan: 82					
COMBINE	40-YD: 5.05	10-YD: 1.77	20-YD: 2.96	BP: —	VJ: 32	BJ: 9'8"	SS: 4.47	3C: 7.51

RONNIE STANLEY
OT / NOTRE DAME

Name: Ronnie Stanley

Ht: 6′5¾″ **Wt:** 312

Hometown/High School: Las Vegas, NV / Bishop Gorman

Class: Redshirt Junior

Number: 78

DOB: March 18, 1994

Career Highlights: Notre Dame Offensive Player of the Year (2015), Consensus All-American (2015), Notre Dame Offensive Lineman of the Year (2014)

Did You Know? Notre Dame has been spoiled at left tackle as Stanley took over for 2014 first-round pick Zack Martin—the last time a player other than Martin or Stanley started at left tackle for the Irish was October 2010.

Fun Fact: Stanley's first love was basketball. He was rated as one of the top power forward recruits in the state of Nevada his senior year of high school.

Ideal Team Fit: While still developing his technique and strength, Stanley has the raw athleticism that has scouts salivating and will make him an attractive prospect for a team in search of a left tackle who specializes in pass protection.

NFL Comparison: D'Brickashaw Ferguson

With Zack Martin entrenched at left tackle, Ronnie Stanley earned the starting right tackle job as a redshirt freshman in 2013 and started all 13 games, pushing incumbent starter Christian Lombard to guard. After Martin graduated (and was drafted in the first round of the 2014 NFL Draft), Stanley moved to the left side in 2014 and started all 13 games as a redshirt sophomore, earning Notre Dame Offensive Lineman of the Year honors. He returned to South Bend for his redshirt junior season in 2015 and again started all 13 games at left tackle, earning consensus All-America and Notre Dame Offensive Player of the Year honors.

STRENGTHS: Looks the part with an ideal frame, girth, and length for the position. Above-average set-up quickness and movement skills to mirror rushers and control himself in space. Doesn't play tight, displaying natural flexibility and bend to open his hips and redirect. Recovers well with terrific reactive athleticism to shuffle, sink, and anchor while maintaining his wide base. Rangy player who can get to the second level and block on the perimeter. Proper pad level off the snap and looks to extend and punch with his reach. Uses his long arms and natural lean to absorb and slow rushers, keeping them from his frame. Durable starting experience, starting every game the last three seasons—39 career starts (26 at left tackle, 13 at right tackle).

WEAKNESSES: High-cut and needs to consistently drop his hips off the snap. Not a power player and lacks ideal functional strength for the position to move bodies in the run game or consistently anchor. Rushers can too easily attack his body and put him on his heels. Sloppy hand placement in his shuffle, struggling to keep his elbows inside to recoil and handle counter moves. Suffers mechanical breakdowns throughout the course of a game, and his focus too easily wavers, leading to false-start penalties and other mistakes. Can get to the second level with ease, but needs to be more aggressive in space, attacking defenders instead of waiting. Room to improve his blocking angles to consistently seal run lanes. Too much finesse in his game and needs to be more of a glass-eater.

SUMMARY: A three-year starter, Stanley started all 39 games the last three seasons for the Irish, first at right and then at left tackle. Boasting an ideal NFL frame for the position, Stanley is a dancing bear with God-given athleticism, long arms and above-average feet to mirror rushers in space. He still needs to develop functional power and fine-tune his mechanics before he's ready for NFL snaps, but his upside and athletic skill-level for a man his size are attractive qualities. While not a top-tier pro prospect due to his inconsistencies, Stanley has intriguing traits and potential at a position of priority in the NFL.

CAREER STATS

SEASON	GP/GS	POS
2012	2/0	*Redshirted*
2013	13/13	RT
2014	13/13	LT
2015	13/13	LT
Career	41/39	26 LT, 13 RT

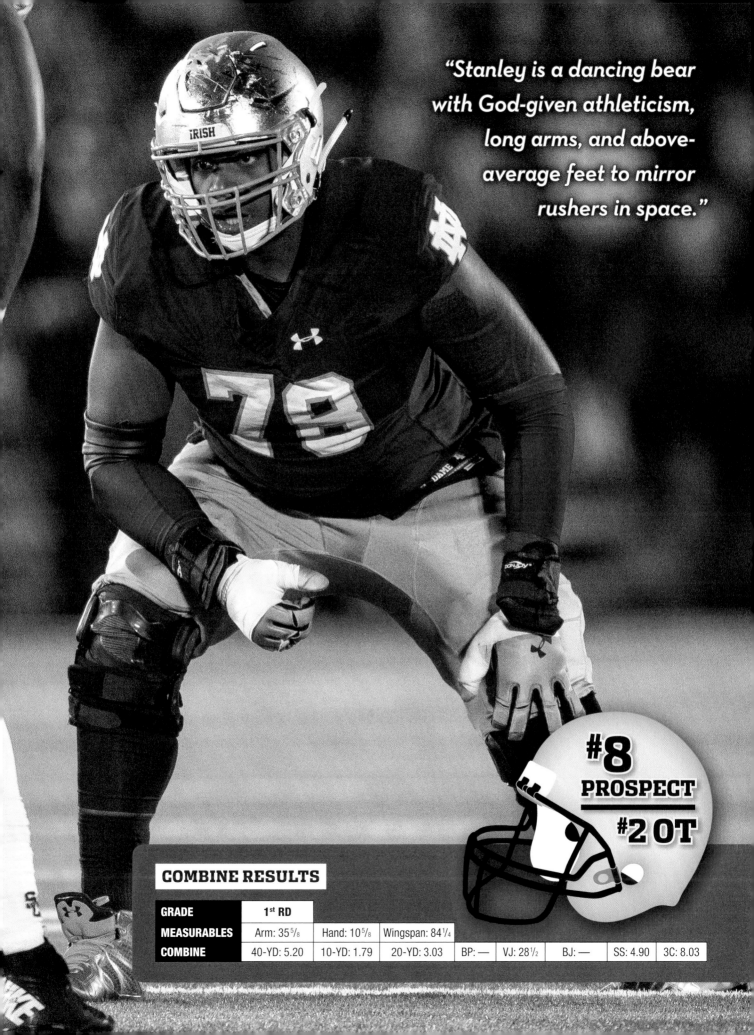

"Stanley is a dancing bear with God-given athleticism, long arms, and above-average feet to mirror rushers in space."

#8 PROSPECT

#2 OT

COMBINE RESULTS

GRADE	1ˢᵗ RD							
MEASURABLES	Arm: 35⅝	Hand: 10⅝	Wingspan: 84¼					
COMBINE	40-YD: 5.20	10-YD: 1.79	20-YD: 3.03	BP: —	VJ: 28½	BJ: —	SS: 4.90	3C: 8.03

JARED GOFF
QB / CALIFORNIA

Name: Jared Goff

Ht: 6'4" **Wt:** 215

Hometown/High School: Novato, CA / Marin Catholic

Class: Junior

Number: 16

DOB: October 14, 1994

Career Highlights: First-Team All-Pac-12 (2015), All-Pac-12 Honorable Mention (2014, 2013)

Did You Know? Only the second Pac-12 passer to throw 3,000-plus yards in his first three seasons and broke Marcus Mariota's conference record for passing touchdowns in a season (43).

Fun Fact: His father (Jeff) was an All-America baseball catcher at Cal and played seven seasons of major league baseball (1990–1996).

Ideal Team Fit: Would benefit from a quick-hitting NFL offense and a play-caller who schemes the passing attack around the weapons on the field, like head coach Hue Jackson of the Cleveland Browns.

NFL Comparison: Mix of Matt Ryan and Teddy Bridgewater

A three-year starter, Jared Goff arrived at Cal with a new coaching staff and a rebuilding program. Goff became the first quarterback in school history to start the season opener as a true freshman in 2013, and despite more losses (23) than wins (14) over his career, he showed immense improvement from year to year, which was reflected in Cal's win-loss records (2013: 1–11, 2014: 5–7, 2015: 8–5). Goff had a record-breaking junior season in 2015, setting new Pac-12 marks for passing yards (4,719) and passing touchdowns (43). He became the first Cal quarterback to earn first-team All-Pac-12 honors since Aaron Rodgers in 2004.

STRENGTHS: Good height for the position with the body type to add weight and fill out. Outstanding feet, set-up quickness, and release, displaying the lower body mechanics to easily buy extra half-seconds, come to balance, and throw in rhythm. Fundamentals don't break down when the play does and is capable of the correct spontaneous decision. Cerebral passing instincts with a strong understanding of anticipation and timing, throwing receivers open. Quick trigger to make all the necessary throws. Improved eye use to hold defenders. Very good placement to give his receivers a chance to catch-and-go. Not a statue, showing enough athleticism to move the pocket and pick up yards as a rusher. Trusts his teammates with a steady demeanor regardless of down-and-distance or what the scoreboard says. Two-year team captain. Started every game the last three seasons (37 career starts). Holds 26 school records, including career passing yards (12,200), TD passes (96), and completions (977).

WEAKNESSES: Currently lacks an ideal build for the position with thin legs. Lacks the arm strength to deliver stick throws without the aid of proper technique and body motion. Deep ball accuracy is very inconsistent and makes his receivers work for it. Bad habit of bypassing tight windows, looking for a "more open" target. Pressure can disrupt his tempo and decision-making, struggling when forced to quicken his release. Doesn't consistently see all 11 defenders. Shotgun, system offense, getting all the play-calls and audibles from the sideline. Average hand size (23 career fumbles).

SUMMARY: Goff has good, not great, physical traits and arm, but his best qualities are his intelligence, pocket mechanics, and ability to self-evaluate. He approaches the game with a professional, unflappable demeanor and is very advanced to see things quickly, process, and execute. Goff has the uncanny ability to stay balanced in his movements and always be in a "ready" position, sliding left or right in rhythm with his eyes downfield. He undoubtedly faces a learning curve at the next level and would benefit from sitting as a rookie, but he has the passing traits and mental process to start early in his NFL career.

CAREER STATS

SEASON	GP/GS	CMP	ATT	PCT	YDS	TDS	INT
2013	12/12	320	531	60.3	3,508	18	10
2014	12/12	316	509	62.1	3,973	35	7
2015	13/13	341	529	64.5	4,719	43	13
Career	37/37	977	1,569	62.3	12,200	96	30

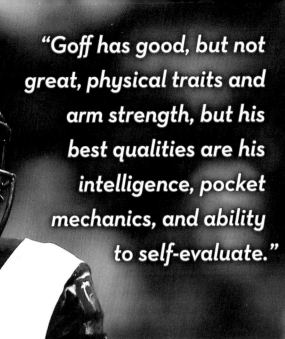

"Goff has good, but not great, physical traits and arm strength, but his best qualities are his intelligence, pocket mechanics, and ability to self-evaluate."

#9 PROSPECT

#1 QB

COMBINE RESULTS

GRADE	1st RD							
MEASURABLES	Arm: 32¾	Hand: 9	Wingspan: 77⅞					
COMBINE	40-YD: 4.82	10-YD: 1.65	20-YD: 2.71	BP: —	VJ: 27	BJ: 9'2"	SS: 4.47	3C: 7.17

CARSON WENTZ
QB / NORTH DAKOTA STATE

Name: Carson Wentz

Ht: 6'5¼" **Wt:** 237

Hometown/High School: Bismarck, ND / Bismarck Central

Class: Redshirt Senior

Number: 11

DOB: December 30, 1992

Career Highlights: FCS All-American (2014), Five-time FCS National Champion (twice as a starter), NCAA Elite 90 recipient and all-conference Honor Roll (2013, 2014, 2015), Senior Bowl (2015)

Did You Know? Wentz faced only one FBS-level opponent in his career, defeating Iowa State in his first career start in August 2014 (18-for-28 for 204 yards, no touchdowns).

Fun Fact: Played wide receiver, linebacker, and safety as a junior in high school because of arm/shoulder problems from baseball, starting at quarterback as a senior.

Ideal Team Fit: Wentz would be an ideal fit with the Dallas Cowboys, who coached him at the Senior Bowl, where he can sit and learn behind Tony Romo. He would also match well with the offense Eagles head coach Doug Pederson wants to run in Philadelphia.

NFL Comparison: Physically enhanced version of Alex Smith

A five-time FCS national champion (twice as a starter), Carson Wentz was a 5'8", 125-pound freshman in high school and didn't start at QB until his senior year, causing him to go vastly under-recruited. Central Michigan was the only FBS program to legitimately show interest, but Wentz stuck to his North Dakota State pledge, where he redshirted in 2011 and served as a backup the next two seasons. He became the starter in 2014 and led the Bison to the FCS national title with a school-record 228 completions and 3,111 passing yards. Wentz started the first six games as a senior before a wrist injury sidelined him for the second half of the 2015 season. He returned for the FCS title game, leading the Bison to its fifth-straight championship.

STRENGTHS: Looks the part with a tall, workable frame. Above-average arm strength to deliver downfield with required velocity and can make all the necessary NFL throws. Tight release, especially for a player with his long arms. Shifts his weight well in the pocket to work through the noise and keep his hand on the trigger, maneuvering under duress with improved footwork. Functional athleticism in the pocket and as a scrambler, avoiding rushers and extending plays (1,028 career rushing yards). Has a pre-snap plan and makes sound decisions. Shows the ability to recognize defensive coverages and blitzes, changing the play at the line with reliable field vision pre- and post-snap. Very smart on and off the field with excellent retention and execution skills. Physically and mentally tough with professional poise and work habits. Great teammate and was an extra coach on the sideline while injured. Consistent winner with a 20–3 career record as a starter and five-time FCS national champion (twice as a starter).

WEAKNESSES: Needs to develop his eye use—locks onto reads, staring down targets and leading defenders. Improved passing anticipation, but still improving his feel for timing routes. Downfield and deep accuracy is inconsistent, leading or underthrowing. Needs to better understand when the play is over and throw the ball away (10 fumbles the last two years). On the move too much, even with a clean pocket, and will attempt throws without setting his base or coming to balance. Lacks ideal starting experience for the position with questions about level of competition—22 of 23 career starts came against FCS competition.

SUMMARY: A two-year starter, Wentz thrived in N.D. State's wide-open offense, taking snaps from under center and shotgun with several pro-style reads, including left-to-right and high-to-low progressions. He didn't consistently face top competition at the FCS level, but performed well in high-pressure situations and has the skill-set and sterling intangibles to be the face of a franchise. Although his experience isn't ideal, Wentz possesses NFL-style tools with his size, athleticism, arm talent, and intelligence to warrant top-10 consideration.

CAREER STATS

SEASON	GP/GS	CMP	ATT	PCT	YDS	TDS	INT
2012	8/0	12	16	75	144	2	0
2013	11/0	22	30	73.3	209	1	0
2014	16/16	228	358	63.7	3,111	25	10
2015	8/7	130	208	62.5	1,651	17	4
Career	43/23	392	612	64.1	5,115	45	14

"Performed well in high-pressure situations. Has the skill-set and sterling intangibles to be the face of a franchise."

#10 PROSPECT

#2 QB

COMBINE RESULTS

GRADE	1ˢᵗ RD							
MEASURABLES	Arm: 33¼	Hand: 10	Wingspan: 78¾					
COMBINE	40-YD: 4.77	10-YD: 1.65	20-YD: 2.75	BP: —	VJ: 30½	BJ: 9'10"	SS: 4.15	3C: 6.86

NOAH SPENCE
DE / EASTERN KENTUCKY

Name: Noah Spence

Ht: 6'2½" **Wt:** 251

Hometown/High School: Harrisburg, PA / Bishop McDevitt

Class: Redshirt Junior

Number: 90

DOB: January 8, 1994

Career Highlights: Senior Bowl (2016), First-Team All-OVC (2015), OVC Defensive Player of the Year (2015), Second-Team All–Big Ten (2013)

Did You Know? Did everything in his power to get clean following his positive drug test and ban from the Big Ten— completed a month-long drug treatment program in the fall of 2014, passed over a dozen drug tests since arriving at EKU and continues to see on-campus counseling.

Fun Fact: Spence's uncle, Phil Spence, was a member of N.C. State's 1974 national championship basketball team and was later drafted by the NBA.

Ideal Team Fit: An explosive edge rusher, Spence is at his best when able to pin his ears back and attack the quarterback. He can put his hand in the dirt, but his skills translate better to a 3-4 scheme where he can operate in space.

NFL Comparison: A smaller Robert Quinn

A five-star recruit out of high school, Noah Spence saw immediate playing time at Ohio State as a true freshman and earned all-conference honors as a sophomore, leading the Buckeyes with eight sacks. However, he was forced to sit out the 2014 season due to multiple failed drug tests and was permanently banned from the Big Ten. Spence strongly considered going pro, but instead decided to transfer to Eastern Kentucky at the FCS level. "I felt like I hadn't proven enough off the field," he said. He started all 11 games as a redshirt junior in 2015 and finished among the FCS leaders in tackles for loss (22.5) and sacks (11.5).

STRENGTHS: Above-average athleticism and initial quickness, reaching his top speed quickly. Launches off the line of scrimmage to dip and win the corner, flattening with natural leverage and a strong plant foot around edge blockers. Outstanding coordination to play on his feet and break down in tight spaces. Rarely caught off-balance due to smooth change-of-direction skills. Flexible body type, lateral quicks and rush moves to cross the face of blockers, using his hands to bounce off jabs and burst into the backfield. Comfortable standing up and dropping in coverage, displaying the range to cover a lot of ground. Work ethic and attitude within the program have never been questioned. Accountable for his past issues, and his former coaches speak highly of him as a person.

WEAKNESSES: Lacks ideal length, and his average height can hinder his backfield vision at times. Needs to use more shock in his hands to jolt blockers at the point of attack. Struggles to consistently convert speed to power. Light anchor and can be moved in the run game. Snap anticipation and awareness for his surroundings need improvement. Comes with a "Buyer Beware" tag due to his history of drug abuse and extensive partying, which earned him a permanent suspension from the Big Ten following a second positive drug test for ecstasy. Shortly after enrolling at EKU, he was arrested for alcohol intoxication and second-degree disorderly conduct (May 2015), although those charges have since been expunged.

SUMMARY: Spence is one of the true wild-cards in this draft class due to his top-10 talent, but heavy baggage off the field. Although his former coaches and teammates speak highly of him as a person, Spence requires monitoring in the NFL due to his background. On the field, he is a slippery rusher with the initial burst, lateral quicks, and natural leverage to threaten the pocket on a regular basis. He is still learning how to put together a consistent pass rush plan, but it's all there athletically and he is comfortable on his feet to cover space. Spence is the best pure pass rusher in the 2016 class, but his draft value will depend on team's comfort level with his past issues.

CAREER STATS

SEASON	GP/GS	TACKLES	TFL	SACKS	FF
2012	11/0	12	1.0	1.0	0
2013	13/13	52	14.5	8.0	1
2014	Suspended				
2015	11/11	63	22.5	11.5	3
Career	35/24	127	38.0	20.5	4

"Spence is one of the true wild-cards in this draft class due to his top-10 talent, but heavy baggage off the field."

#11 PROSPECT

#3 DE

COMBINE RESULTS

GRADE	1ˢᵗ RD							
MEASURABLES	Arm: 33	Hand: 10¾	Wingspan: 79¾					
COMBINE	40-YD: 4.80	10-YD: 1.61	20-YD: 2.75	BP: 25	VJ: 35	BJ: 10'1"	SS: 4.35	3C: 7.21

JAYLON SMITH
LB / NOTRE DAME

Name: Jaylon Smith

Ht: 6′2″ **Wt:** 223

Hometown/High School: Fort Wayne, IN / Bishop Luers

Class: Junior

Number: 9

DOB: June 14, 1995

Career Highlights: Butkus Award (2015), All-American (2015), Notre Dame Defensive Player of the Year Award (2015), All-American (2014), Notre Dame Defensive Player of the Year (2014), Freshman All-American (2013)

Did You Know? Notre Dame head coach Brian Kelly considers Smith the best player he's ever been around: "I haven't coached a player like him before, period."

Fun Fact: Quit the basketball team his senior year in high school in order to take a part-time position at Burger King—not because he needed the money, but because he "wanted a different experience."

Ideal Team Fit: Any team that uses linebackers and is not scared off by the medicals. All 32 teams will be interested in Smith's freakish ability and versatility to play any linebacker spot in either 3-4 or 4-3 schemes.

NFL Comparison: Bobby Wagner

The first freshman linebacker at Notre Dame to start the season opener since 1995, Jaylon Smith started all 13 games in 2013 and separated himself early as a player who was wired differently than everyone else. He started every game in 2014 as a sophomore and led the team with 112 tackles, earning Notre Dame Defensive Player of the Year honors. Smith again hit the triple-digit tackle mark in 2015 as a junior with 114 stops to earn the Butkus Award as the Nation's top linebacker. He didn't miss a start for the Irish the past three seasons (39 straight starts), but in a cruel twist of fate, Smith suffered a devastating knee injury in the bowl game.

STRENGTHS: A greased-up athlete with rare twitch for the position. Explosive lateral agility and secondary quickness to unhook himself from blocks and burst to the ball. Plays loose, low, and balanced to collect himself in space and easily change directions. Tremendous closing speed in pursuit with the acceleration to stay stride-for-stride in coverage. Assignment sound, arriving to the spot with proper timing. Fast eyes to see plays develop, rarely losing sight of the ball. Anchors well at the point of attack, leveraging at the hole to attack run lanes. Navigates well through a crowd due to his vision, instincts, and reactive athleticism. Shows burst as a pass rusher and blitzer, staying in control of his movements. Active and rangy tackler with strong hands and wrists to make stops. Experienced making calls and orchestrating the defense. Mature, unselfish leader and team captain.

WEAKNESSES: Lacks elite length, power, and shed technique and can be engulfed near the line of scrimmage. Will take some false steps and needs to add a bit of discipline. Needs to tweak his strike zone and tackling mechanics, preferring to hug-and-slam instead of spearing and driving. Needs to do a better job finding the ball in coverage once his back is turned. Not a detailed pass rusher right now and needs to better anticipate blockers. Suffered a left knee injury that required surgery (January 2016) to repair a torn ACL and LCL.

SUMMARY: A three-year starter, Smith started at outside linebacker in Notre Dame's 3-4 scheme in 2013 before moving to weak-side linebacker the past two seasons when the Irish went to a 4-3 base. A special athlete for the position, Smith jumps off the screen with his sudden pursuit speed and twitchy movements, which complements his quick-thinking play style. He recognizes things quickly and sniffs out plays, putting himself in correct position to close ground. Smith does have room to improve his discipline and anticipation, but he is dripping with natural talent and intangibles—the type of playmaker you wind up and let loose. Smith is one of the best players in the 2016 class, but his landing spot in the draft will depend on his rehab and recovery.

CAREER STATS

SEASON	GP/GS	TACKLES	TFL	SACKS	FF	INT
2013	13/13	67	6.5	0.0	1	0
2014	13/13	112	9.0	3.5	1	0
2015	13/13	114	9.0	1.0	1	0
Career	39/39	293	24.5	4.5	3	0

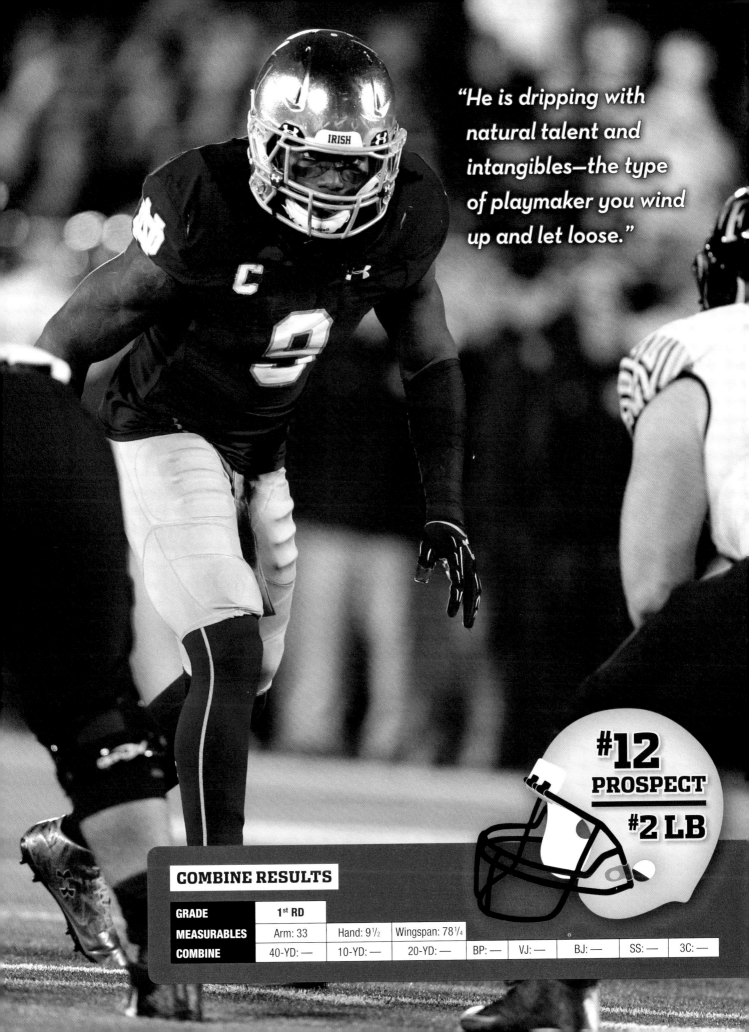

"He is dripping with natural talent and intangibles—the type of playmaker you wind up and let loose."

#12 PROSPECT

#2 LB

COMBINE RESULTS

GRADE	1ST RD							
MEASURABLES	Arm: 33	Hand: 9½	Wingspan: 78¼					
COMBINE	40-YD: —	10-YD: —	20-YD: —	BP: —	VJ: —	BJ: —	SS: —	3C: —

MACKENSIE ALEXANDER
CB / CLEMSON

Name: Mackensie Alexander

Ht: 5'10⅜" **Wt:** 190

Hometown/High School: Immokalee, FL / Immokalee

Class: Redshirt Sophomore

Number: 2

DOB: November 12, 1993

Career Highlights: First-Team All-ACC (2015), Freshman All-American (2014), All-ACC Honorable Mention (2014)

Did You Know? Although his career production is unimpressive, opposing quarterbacks completed only 24.5% of passes in 2015 when targeting the receiver he was covering.

Fun Fact: Has a twin brother (Mackenro) who began his career as an Auburn defensive back before transferring to the JUCO ranks. He plans to play the 2015 season at South Florida.

Ideal Team Fit: Alexander will face a learning curve in the NFL as he adjusts his cover technique and anticipation, but all the traits are there for him to start for a press-man scheme.

NFL Comparison: A smaller Josh Norman

Usually cornerback prospects with zero career interceptions aren't in the conversion to be first-round picks, but Mackensie Alexander is the exception, mostly because he was seldom targeted by opposing offenses. After redshirting in 2013 due to a groin injury, Alexander earned a starting cornerback job as a redshirt freshman in 2014 and set a school record for snaps by a freshman, collecting 21 tackles and six passes defended to earn Freshman All-America honors. He started 14 games for the ACC champions in 2015 as a sophomore and posted similar production with 23 tackles and five passes defended.

STRENGTHS: Quick-footed in his transition with the speed to match receivers off the line of scrimmage. Fluid hips with the lower body muscle fibers to spring in any direction. Nimble drive process to click-and-close. Uses his body to cut off routes, understanding how to leverage the field and sideline. Keeps an eye in the backfield to jump routes and intercept angles. Highly physical for the position in both coverage and run support. Very good high-to-low tackler downhill, throwing his body around and beating blockers to the spot. Cocky, brash, and competes with an attitude, playing mind games with receivers. Applies coaching and is dedicated to his craft. Innately motivated, with a fire for competition. Battle tested over 27 starts, usually covering the opponent's top receiving threat.

WEAKNESSES: Lacks elite size and arm length for the position. Played mostly press-bail technique in college, flipping his hips early in the play, which caused him to get turned around instead of staying square to the receiver. Not as comfortable in off-coverage and still developing his coverage anticipation and understanding of route concepts. Struggles to locate the ball once he takes his eyes off the backfield and needs to improve his feel with his back to the QB. Suspect ball skills and will leave production on the field (no interceptions). Throws his body around, but prefers to strike with his shoulder instead of wrapping up. Puts too much pressure on himself to be the best and needs to keep his emotions in check. Marches to his own beat with a guarded personality.

SUMMARY: A two-year starter at Clemson, Alexander played mostly press-man coverage and was left on an island, relying primarily on bail technique. He didn't record a pick in college, but was rarely targeted and didn't give up a TD the last 24 games, dating back to September of his freshman season. He smothers in man coverage due to his lower body fluidity and quick reflexes, but needs to improve his route anticipation and ball skills, especially in off coverage. He plays with contagious swagger and confidence, working hard to get in the heads of wide receivers. Although still developing in several key areas, Alexander is wired right for the position and should start very early in his NFL career.

CAREER STATS

SEASON	GP/GS	TACKLES	TFL	SACKS	FF	PASS DEF	INT
2013	*Redshirted*						
2014	13/13	21	2.0	0.0	0	6	0
2015	15/14	23	2.0	0.0	0	5	0
Career	28/27	44	4.0	0.0	0	11	0

"He plays with contagious swagger and confidence, working hard to get in the heads of wide receivers."

#13 PROSPECT

#1 CB

COMBINE RESULTS

GRADE	1ST RD							
MEASURABLES	Arm: 31³/₈	Hand: 9¹/₈	Wingspan: 75¹/₂					
COMBINE	40-YD: —	10-YD: —	20-YD: —	BP: 11	VJ: —	BJ: —	SS: —	3C: —

REGGIE RAGLAND
LB / ALABAMA

Name: Reggie Ragland

Ht: 6'1¼" **Wt:** 247

Hometown/High School: Madison, AL / Bob Jones

Class: Senior

Number: 19

DOB: September 14, 1993

Career Highlights: Senior Bowl (2016), CFP National Champion (2016), SEC Defensive Player of the Year (2015), First-Team All-SEC (2015), Unanimous All-American (2015), First-Team All-SEC (2014)

Did You Know? Never afraid of competition, Ragland requested to play outside linebacker at the 2016 Senior Bowl in order to show NFL scouts he is a complete player.

Fun Fact: With a crowded linebacker depth chart when Ragland arrived in Tuscaloosa, he and Saban discussed moving to tight end to get him on the field.

Ideal Team Fit: Although unproven as a consistent cover man, Ragland is NFL-ready as a punishing, instinctive run defender, ideally suited as an inside linebacker in a 3-4 scheme like the New York Jets or Chicago Bears.

NFL Comparison: David Harris

Since 2010, Nick Saban has had three inside linebackers drafted top-25 (Rolando McClain, Dont'a Hightower, and C.J. Mosley), and Reggie Ragland could be the fourth in April. With a logjam at linebacker when he arrived in Tuscaloosa, Ragland was a valuable reserve and special teamer as a freshman and sophomore. With Mosley leaving for the NFL after the 2013 season, Ragland won the starting weak-side inside linebacker job and finished second on the team with 95 tackles and 10.5 tackles for loss. He returned for his senior season in 2015 and led the team in tackles (102) and was named the SEC Defensive Player of the Year.

STRENGTHS: Well-strapped together with tough body armor, thick bubble, and long arms. Not an elite speed player, but plays with reactive athleticism, closing burst, and lateral quickness to avoid second-level blocks. Explosive striker to separate man from ball, unlocking his hips and finishing. Technically sound wrap tackler with strong wrists and hands. Quick eyes to diagnose and attack to see plays develop and plan accordingly. Makes all the defensive calls and is an extra coach on the field. Disciplined and prepared, not falling for fakes and rarely making mental mistakes. Loves watching film and has developed his football recognition skills. Active blitzer and will put his hand on the ground in passing situations, shaving blocks around the corner. Violent play style and doesn't stay blocked for long. High effort player with a love for football.

WEAKNESSES: Overaggressive pursuit angles and needs to better throttle down in space to break down at the contact point. Hyper-focused run defender and will leave his eyes in the backfield too long at times, causing him to be late in coverage. Trusts what he sees, but often too patient. Needs to widen his vision to protect from cut blocks, pick up crossers, and better recognize routes. Learns more by repetition. Out-matched trying to stick with slot receivers down the field in coverage. Violent play style leads to durability questions.

SUMMARY: A two-year starter, Ragland lined up primarily at the weak-side inside linebacker position, playing the same role as Hightower and Mosley in Nick Saban's scheme, also putting his hand on the ground as an edge rusher when Alabama went to four-man fronts. He is an excellent point-of-attack player with good play speed, and it's no coincidence that he's always around the ball with his ability to diagnose plays. Ragland can be overaggressive at times, which leads to misses, but he is the hardest hitter in this class and flashes violence in his hands to detach himself from blocks. Although he needs polish in coverage, Ragland is a garbage man in the run game, working well through the trash to shut down the run.

CAREER STATS

SEASON	GP/GS	TACKLES	TFL	SACKS	FF	INT
2012	11/0	8	0.0	0.0	1	0
2013	13/0	17	0.5	0.0	0	0
2014	14/13	95	10.5	1.5	1	1
2015	15/15	102	6.5	2.5	2	0
Career	53/28	222	17.5	4.0	4	1

"Ragland is a garbage man in the run game, working well through the trash to shut down the run."

#14 PROSPECT

#3 LB

COMBINE RESULTS

GRADE	1ˢᵗ RD							
MEASURABLES	Arm: 32	Hand: 9⅞	Wingspan: 77¾					
COMBINE	40-YD: 4.72	10-YD: 1.65	20-YD: 2.75	BP: —	VJ: 31½	BJ: 9'8"	SS: 4.28	3C: —

VERNON HARGREAVES III
CB / FLORIDA

Name: Vernon Hargreaves III

Ht: 5′10½″ **Wt:** 204

Hometown/High School: Tampa, FL / Wharton

Class: Junior

Number: 1

DOB: June 3, 1995

Career Highlights: Thorpe Award Finalist (2015), First-Team All-SEC (2015), All-American (2015), First-Team All-SEC (2014), All-American (2014), First-Team All-SEC (2013), All-American (2013)

Did You Know? His father (Vernon Jr.) was an All-America linebacker at UConn and has been a longtime football coach, currently the linebackers coach at Arkansas.

Fun Fact: Hargreaves has a chance to become the 25th Florida Gator selected in the first round over the last 20 years. Only three programs have more first-rounders in that time.

Ideal Team Fit: Similar to when he arrived at Florida, Hargreaves will be an instant contributor in the NFL as either an inside or outside corner who can play both press and off-coverage.

NFL Comparison: Joe Haden

One of the top defensive backs to enter the NFL from Gainesville, Vernon Hargreaves earned All-SEC and All-America honors each of his three seasons at Florida and was a finalist for the Thorpe Award in 2015. As the top prep player in the 2013 recruiting class, he had his choice of schools, committing to the Gators and seeing immediate playing time as a true freshman with three interceptions. Hargreaves started 25 games the last two seasons and combined for 24 passes defended and seven interceptions.

STRENGTHS: Adequate build for the position. Above-average athleticism with controlled play speed and footwork. Good drive mechanics and throttles down well to make stops. Smooth pedal and quick feet to shadow receivers with his body control and vision always in sync. Excellent secondary burst to close on routes and as a blitzer. Observant and understands route indicators, recognizing things quickly to react. Usually has very good timing, understanding how to properly bait throws. Tougher, stronger, and more physical than he looks with the ability to finish tackles by himself. Leverages the field well and understands angles. Innate competitive nature and very aggressive at the catch point. NFL-level ball skills and return skills, averaging 19.1 yards per interception return. Plays with contagious swagger and rarely gets bored. Possesses the requisite toughness (mentally and physically) for the next level.

WEAKNESSES: Shorter than ideal and his lack of length and size will show up at times, especially against good-sized targets. Needs to develop his functional strength to be a sound run defender. Will get himself in trouble trying to rip the ball out instead of making the sure tackle. Needs to improve his cushion and spacing in coverage, allowing his eyes to spend too much time in the backfield and losing track of his man. Needs to do a better job getting his head turned to locate. Needs to keep his aggression in check to avoid late hits and biting on double-moves. Limited return experience on special teams. Didn't miss much time at Florida due to injury, but his lack of size leads to durability concerns.

SUMMARY: A three-year starter, Hargreaves quickly established himself as one of the SEC's top defensive backs as a freshman and played at a high level the last three seasons, often against the top opposing wide receiver. The son of a coach, he grew up with football and plays the game with a competitive appetite, coaching his teammates and taking a leadership role at a young age. Hargreaves plays with a decisive reactor to maintain proper positioning and make plays on the ball (38 career passes defended), but his inconsistent spacing and lack of size show up too often. Despite his shortcomings, Hargreaves is above average in three main areas for the position: play speed, instincts, and competitive toughness, like another former Florida cornerback, Joe Haden.

CAREER STATS

SEASON	GP/GS	TACKLES	TFL	SACKS	FF	PASS DEF	INT
2013	12/10	38	0.0	0.0	0	14	3
2014	12/12	50	2.0	0.0	0	16	3
2015	13/13	33	1.0	0.0	1	8	4
Career	37/35	121	3.0	0.0	1	38	10

"Hargreaves is above-average in three main areas for the position: play speed, instincts, and competitive toughness."

#15 PROSPECT

#2 CB

COMBINE RESULTS

GRADE	1st RD								
MEASURABLES	Arm: 30⅝	Hand: 8⅛	Wingspan: 72⅞						
COMBINE	40-YD: 4.50	10-YD: 1.58	20-YD: 2.62	BP: 15	VJ: 39	BJ: 10'10"	SS: 3.98	3C: —

SHAQ LAWSON
DE / CLEMSON

Name: Shaq Lawson

Ht: 6′2⅝″ **Wt:** 269

Hometown/High School: Central, SC / Daniel

Class: Junior

Number: 90

DOB: June 17, 1994

Career Highlights: Runner-up ACC Defensive Player of the Year (2015), Consensus All-American (2015), First-Team All-ACC (2015)

Did You Know? If Lawson is drafted in the top 25, it will mark the first time in school history that Clemson will have three straight years with at least one top-25 draft pick (2015: Vic Beasley; 2014: Sammy Watkins).

Fun Fact: His first love was on the basketball court, and he always hoped to follow in the footsteps of his father and uncle who played college basketball.

Ideal Team Fit: A leverage-based edge defender who wins with instincts, power, and quickness, ideally suited at left defensive end in a 4-3 base like the Philadelphia Eagles or Tampa Bay Buccaneers.

NFL Comparison: Pernell McPhee

From D.W. High School to Clemson, Shaq Lawson followed the same path as DeAndre Hopkins and several others who are currently playing in the NFL. After a stop at military school due to academics, Lawson was stuck behind Vic Beasley and Corey Crawford on the depth chart, but Lawson was still able to make an impact as a reserve underclassman. Despite only one combined start as a freshman and sophomore, he posted double-digit tackles for loss both seasons. Lawson finally received his chance to be a full-time starter as a junior in 2015 and was runner-up for ACC Defensive Player of the Year with an NCAA-best 25.5 tackles for loss, adding 60 tackles and 12.5 sacks to earn first-team All-ACC and All-America honors.

STRENGTHS: Proportionate upper- and lower-body thickness. Quick initial step with the lateral agility and knee bend to rush with low pad level. Stays coordinated in his rush sequence, using a variety of spin and power arm moves to beat blocks. Resets his vision well on the move to find the ball carrier, coming to balance to make stops in small spaces. Active, heavy hands to stack the edge, fight off blockers' jabs, and create push with his upper body. Disciplined versus the run, holding the edge and leveraging blocks with an iron shoulder and body flexibility. Heavy striker who drives through his hips, bringing his legs with him. Takes well to coaching and praised for his football intelligence ("one of the easiest guys I've ever coached," according to Tigers head coach Dabo Swinney). Led the nation in tackles for loss (25.5) last year and finished his career with 46.5.

WEAKNESSES: Only average height and length for the position. Not a twitchy or naturally explosive athlete to win the corner on burst alone. Needs to quicken his recoil and get his hands back to better halt runners in his gap. While balanced and agile to drop and move in reverse, he lacks the range and redirection traits to consistently cover in space. Only one season of starting experience. Durability needs to be vetted following a sprained MCL in his left knee in the Orange Bowl (December 2015), along with his history of sore shoulders, requiring a brace on his right shoulder.

SUMMARY: Despite losing eight defensive starters prior to the 2015 season, Clemson's defense ranked top-10 nationally, and Lawson was a substantial reason for that, leading the country in tackles for loss in his only year as a starter. He is intelligent and powerful, using leverage, flexibility, and savvy to secure the edge and be equally productive versus the run and the pass. Lawson isn't a long-armed, twitchy athlete who will capture the corner on speed alone, but his efficient pass-rush process and ball awareness will force NFL offensive tackles to prepare for his skill-set.

CAREER STATS

SEASON	GP/GS	TACKLES	TFL	SACKS	FF
2013	13/0	35	10.0	4.0	0
2014	13/1	44	11.0	3.5	1
2015	15/15	60	25.5	12.5	1
Career	41/16	139	46.5	20.0	2

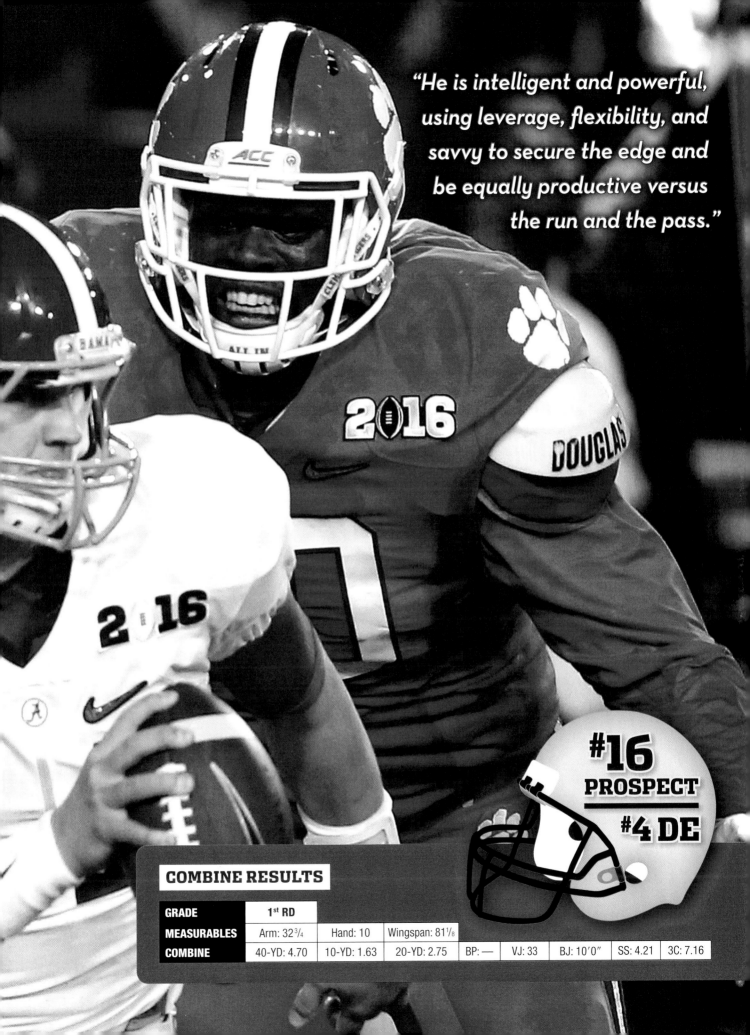

"He is intelligent and powerful, using leverage, flexibility, and savvy to secure the edge and be equally productive versus the run and the pass."

#16 PROSPECT
#4 DE

COMBINE RESULTS

GRADE	1st RD							
MEASURABLES	Arm: 32¾	Hand: 10	Wingspan: 81⅛					
COMBINE	40-YD: 4.70	10-YD: 1.63	20-YD: 2.75	BP: —	VJ: 33	BJ: 10'0"	SS: 4.21	3C: 7.16

DARRON LEE
LB / OHIO STATE

Name: Darron Lee

Ht: 6' 3/4" **Wt:** 232

Hometown/High School: New Albany, OH / New Albany

Class: Redshirt Sophomore

Number: 43

DOB: October 18, 1995

Career Highlights: Second-Team All–Big Ten (2015), CFP National Champion (2015), Sugar Bowl Defensive MVP (2015)

Did You Know? Urban Meyer admits that he "didn't see it" with the athletic, lanky Lee in high school, but credits defensive coordinator Luke Fickell for recognizing the potential.

Fun Fact: Lee's mother (Candice) is a weekend anchor and weekday reporter for WCMH Channel 4, the local NBC affiliate in Columbus.

Ideal Team Fit: Lee has the skill-set ideal for a weak-side linebacker role in a 4-3 scheme like the Cincinnati Bengals or Atlanta Falcons. He will be a stand-out on special teams while competing for a starting role as an NFL rookie.

NFL Comparison: Kwon Alexander

A 195-pound quarterback in high school, Buckeyes coaches weren't sure where Darron Lee would play in college, but they had the foresight to know he could play. After redshirting as a scout-team safety, he earned the strong-side linebacker job as a redshirt freshman in 2014, filling the shoes of Ryan Shazier and collecting 81 tackles, 16.5 tackles for loss, 7.5 sacks, and a pair of interceptions. Lee started all 13 games in 2015 as a redshirt sophomore, finishing with 66 tackles, 11 tackles for loss, and 4.5 sacks to earn second-team All–Big Ten honors.

STRENGTHS: Above-average range, speed, and athleticism. Unlocks his hips to instantly accelerate and close like a runaway train. Makes himself skinny and shoots through gaps on the line of scrimmage. Needs to do it consistently, but flashes violence in his hands to punch, lock out, and keep himself free from blocks. Explosive tackler and doesn't need a runway, striking low and leading with his shoulder. Performs with an instant reactor and diagnoses play speed well. Quick-minded, recognizing tendencies and play-calling trends—sees it on film and throughout the course of a game. Smooth hips to turn and run in coverage. Agile pass rusher to blitz, stunt, and loop. Self-assured presence on and off the field with a competitive swagger that seems to shine when the lights are the brightest. Versatile experience as a blitzer, run defender, and cover man—often lined up across from the slot receiver in coverage. Started every game the past two seasons with consistent production.

WEAKNESSES: Leaner-than-ideal features for the position with a narrow torso and maxed out build. Physical mind-set with pop in his hands, but lacks ideal play strength to consistently unglue himself from blocks—stonewalled by offensive linemen and needs to improve his take-on technique to stay clean and gain body position. Overaggressive angles and needs to better come to balance and break down while in motion. Needs to mix up his moves and show a better plan as a blitzer. Only two full seasons at linebacker and still learning different nuances of the position. Doesn't have an indestructible body type.

SUMMARY: A two-year starter in Ohio State's versatile 4-3 base defense, Lee redshirted as a safety, but added muscle and moved to linebacker, playing the "walkout" role so he was asked to cover, blitz, and consistently play in space. Lee is a fantastic athlete with long arms and aggressive hands, but needs to develop his functional strength to consistently stack-and-shed at the line of scrimmage and keep himself clean. Although he is still young in linebacker years, he is a high character competitor, playing with sky-high confidence and natural football instincts to pick things up quickly. Lee is a versatile run-and-hit linebacker with an attacking mind-set that fits today's NFL.

CAREER STATS

SEASON	GP/GS	TACKLES	TFL	SACKS	FF	INT
2013			*Redshirted*			
2014	15/15	81	16.5	7.5	1	2
2015	13/13	66	11.0	4.5	0	1
Career	28/28	147	27.5	12.0	1	3

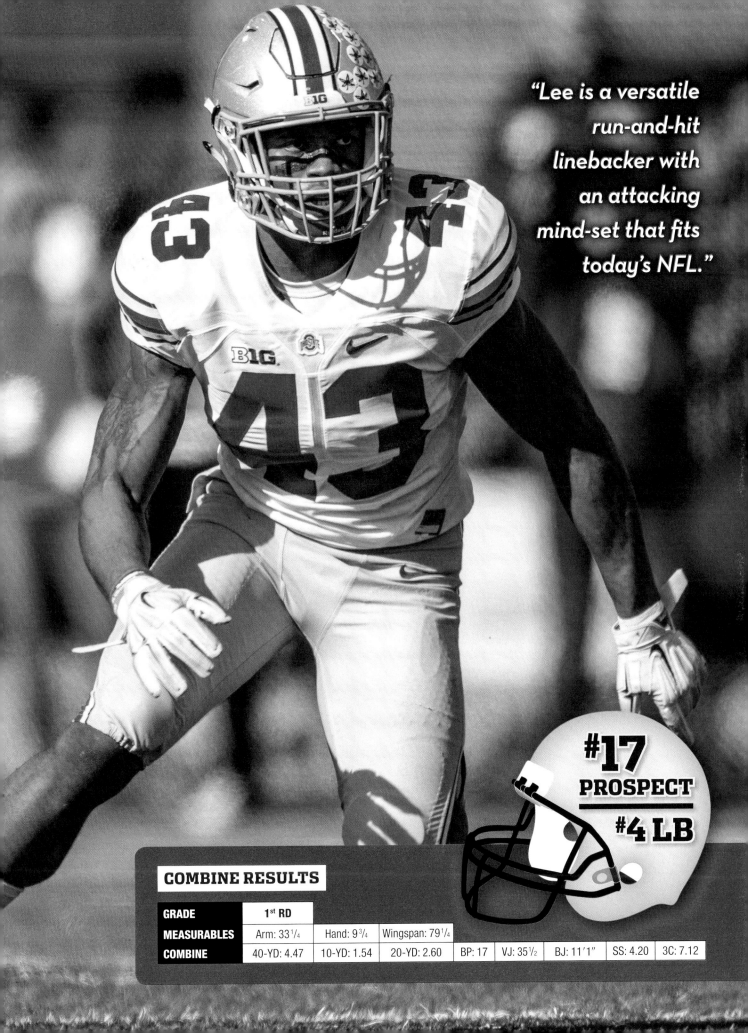

"Lee is a versatile run-and-hit linebacker with an attacking mind-set that fits today's NFL."

#17 PROSPECT

#4 LB

COMBINE RESULTS

GRADE	1ST RD							
MEASURABLES	Arm: 33¼	Hand: 9¾	Wingspan: 79¼					
COMBINE	40-YD: 4.47	10-YD: 1.54	20-YD: 2.60	BP: 17	VJ: 35½	BJ: 11'1"	SS: 4.20	3C: 7.12

SHELDON RANKINS
DT / LOUISVILLE

Name: Sheldon Rankins

Ht: 6′1⅛″ **Wt:** 299

Hometown/High School: Covington, GA / Eastside

Class: Senior

Number: 98

DOB: April 2, 1994

Career Highlights: Senior Bowl (2016), Second-Team All-ACC (2015), Third-Team All-ACC (2014)

Did You Know? Rankins is attempting to join Amobi Okoye (10th overall, 2007) as the only defensive linemen from Louisville drafted in the top 20.

Fun Fact: Clemson head coach Dabo Swinney was highly impressed with Rankins when they played the Cardinals: "That No. 98 they got is probably as good a player as we're going to see…he's probably a high draft pick."

Ideal Team Fit: Whether one-gapping or two-gapping, lining up inside or out, Rankins has the skill-set that supersedes scheme. He is best-suited for a three-technique role for a four-man front like the Carolina Panthers.

NFL Comparison: Kawann Short

Charlie Strong lured Sheldon Rankins to Louisville, where he developed into one of the most talented, yet unrecognized defensive-line prospects in the country. He saw part-time playing time as a freshman and sophomore, starting three games his first two seasons and combining for four sacks. Rankins earned a full-time starting job at left defensive end as a junior and led the team in tackles for loss (13.5) and sacks (8), adding 53 tackles to earn third-team All-ACC honors. He started all 13 games in 2015 as a senior and finished second on the team in tackles for loss (13) and sacks (6), earning second-team All-ACC honors.

STRENGTHS: Meaty thighs, broad shoulders, and proportionate thickness. Good snap quickness to attack gaps and push the pocket. Generates force with initial step and heavy hands to load up and jar blockers off balance. Grip strength to set the edge and hold the point versus power. Instinctive vision to anticipate and accurately track the ball, seeing through blockers. Redirects well for his size with the hip action to collect himself on the move and adjust to moving targets. Breaks down well in smaller spaces and stays on his feet. Improved pass-rush skills and production (18 career sacks). Uses his length and large hands to knock down throws at the line of scrimmage (six career passes defended and two interceptions). Determined chaser with the hustle to catch ball carriers from behind. Well-versed at several defensive-line techniques in multiple fronts. Senior captain and his coaches speak highly of his work ethic, playing temperament, and focus. Louisville defensive coordinator Todd Grantham said, "I think he can play a long time at the next level."

WEAKNESSES: Frame near maxed out with some bad weight in his midsection. Often the last lineman to move off the ball and needs to improve his snap anticipation. Active hands, but still developing his pass-rush moves and needs to improve his punch placement. Doesn't always rush with a plan and lacks consistent move-to-move transition. Will stand up at times and needs to play with lower pad level.

SUMMARY: A two-year starter at defensive end in Louisville's hybrid 3-4 scheme, Rankins also saw playing time at nose tackle, one-technique, and three-technique in the Cardinals' multiple fronts. He is a balanced athlete for his size with the physical presence and hand strength to press blockers off his frame, create separation, and disrupt the backfield. Rankins keeps his eyes trained on the ball and not only prefers to use his hands, but he also understands different tactics to shed and be a playmaker versus the run and pass. He will see playing time early in his career and compete for starting reps.

CAREER STATS

SEASON	GP/GS	TACKLES	TFL	SACKS	FF
2012	10/2	7	1.0	1.0	0
2013	10/1	15	4.0	3.0	1
2014	13/13	53	13.5	8.0	1
2015	13/13	58	13.0	6.0	0
Career	46/29	133	31.5	18.0	2

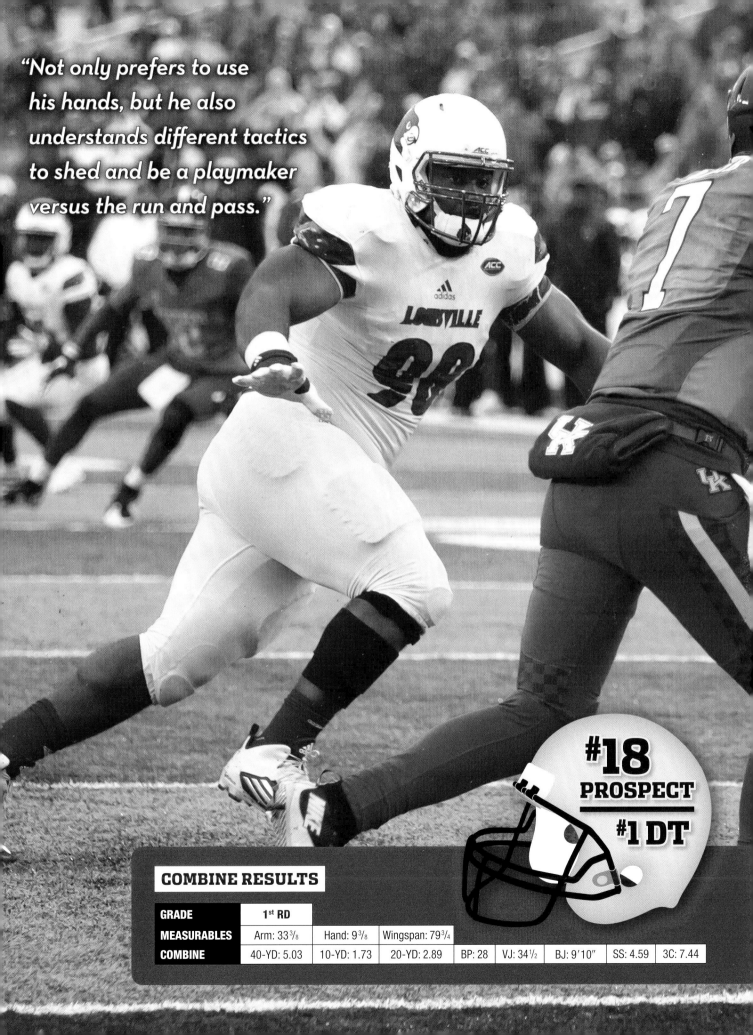

"Not only prefers to use his hands, but he also understands different tactics to shed and be a playmaker versus the run and pass."

#18 PROSPECT

#1 DT

COMBINE RESULTS

GRADE	1ST RD							
MEASURABLES	Arm: 33 3/8	Hand: 9 3/8	Wingspan: 79 3/4					
COMBINE	40-YD: 5.03	10-YD: 1.73	20-YD: 2.89	BP: 28	VJ: 34 1/2	BJ: 9'10"	SS: 4.59	3C: 7.44

JARRAN REED
DT / ALABAMA

Name: Jarran Reed

Ht: 6'2⅞" **Wt:** 307

Hometown/High School: Goldsboro, NC / Goldsboro

Class: Senior

Number: 90

DOB: December 16, 1992

Career Highlights: Senior Bowl (2016), CFP National Champions (2016)

Did You Know? Led all Alabama defensive linemen in tackles each of the last two years, which accurately reflects his impact versus the run.

Fun Fact: A linebacker recruit out of high school, Reed didn't receive any offers from major programs and was set to play at Division-II Fayetteville State.

Ideal Team Fit: A well-built, nimble nose tackle capable of shutting down the run as a nose tackle in a 3-4 scheme or playing various techniques in a four-man front.

NFL Comparison: Dan Williams

From Hargrave Military Academy to East Mississippi Community College to Alabama, it took a winding road, but Jarran Reed eventually landed in the SEC. At different points in his recruitment, he was committed to North Carolina, Ole Miss, and Florida, but academic issues sidelined those plans, forcing him to return to Community College for the 2013 season. Reed committed to the Crimson Tide for the 2014 season, starting the final 13 games, recording 55 tackles, 6.5 tackles for loss, and one sack. Reed considered going pro, but returned to Tuscaloosa for his senior season and finished with 57 tackles, 4.5 tackles for loss, and a sack.

STRENGTHS: Built like a vending machine with arms due to his strong trunk and thick hips. Immovable object at the point of attack and rarely put in reverse, stacking with a strong upper body to control blocks. Initial pop to generate movement off the snap and push the pocket when attempting to pass rush. Moves well for his size with the lateral agility to stunt, drop his hips, and bend around bodies. Physical hands and improved shed technique, taking advantage of body angles, leverage, and leaning blockers. High tackle numbers (112 the past two seasons) due to his instincts and patience versus the run. Knack for blocking sight lines and knocking down passes at the line of scrimmage (seven career passes defended). Tough-minded to do the dirty work in the trenches with experience at nose guard and several defensive-line techniques. Reliable competitor and has shown the ability to overcome setbacks.

WEAKNESSES: Average overall range and pursuit speed with minimal impact outside the hashes. Good effort in pursuit but will tire quickly. Limited pass-rush skills and doesn't show the functional moves to beat blockers and infiltrate the pocket. Not a three-down player in every scheme. Will stand up at times off the snap, negating his ability to two-gap. Admittedly made a "childish mistake" after a July 2014 DUI, and his off-field decision-making needs to be investigated.

SUMMARY: A two-year starter in Alabama's 3-4 base defense, Reed lined up mostly as the nose tackle, but also moved to various inside positions between the zero and five technique spots. He is balanced to absorb contact at the point of attack, holding his ground with a stout anchor and fierce hand work. Reed isn't a rangy player, but is a smooth athlete for his size, scraping down the line of scrimmage and pushing the pocket with initial momentum. He has a small radius of impact, but he's very effective in that small area. Although he won't sell many jerseys, Reed is the type of run defender every NFL team would love to add to the rotation.

CAREER STATS

SEASON	GP/GS	TACKLES	TFL	SACKS	FF
2014	14/13	55	6.5	1.0	0
2015	15/15	57	4.5	1.0	0
Career	29/28	112	11.0	2.0	0

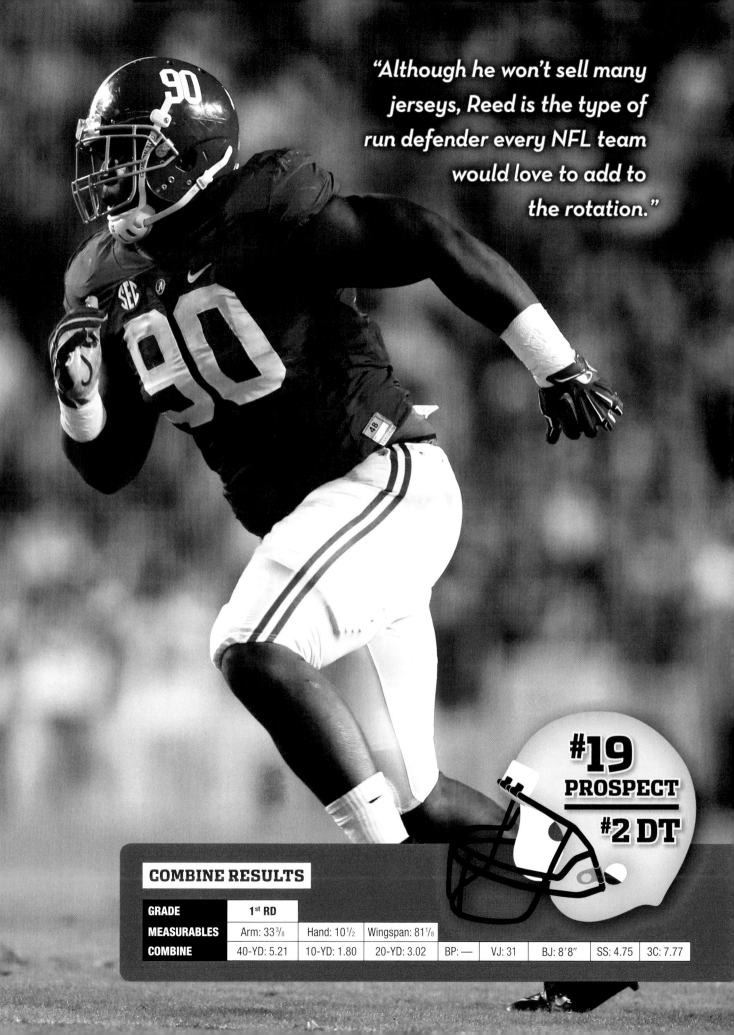

"Although he won't sell many jerseys, Reed is the type of run defender every NFL team would love to add to the rotation."

#19 PROSPECT
#2 DT

COMBINE RESULTS

GRADE	1ST RD							
MEASURABLES	Arm: 33³/₈	Hand: 10¹/₂	Wingspan: 81¹/₈					
COMBINE	40-YD: 5.21	10-YD: 1.80	20-YD: 3.02	BP: —	VJ: 31	BJ: 8'8"	SS: 4.75	3C: 7.77

CODY WHITEHAIR
OG / KANSAS STATE

Name: Cody Whitehair

Ht: 6′3¾″ **Wt:** 301

Hometown/High School: Abilene, KS / Abilene

Class: Redshirt Senior

Number: 55

DOB: July 11, 1992

Career Highlights: Senior Bowl (2016), Second-Team All–Big 12 (2015), Second-Team All–Big 12 (2014), Second-Team All–Big 12 (2013), All–Big 12 Honorable Mention (2012)

Did You Know? Although his preference is to line up inside at guard, Whitehair allowed only two sacks as a senior left tackle in 2015.

Fun Fact: If chosen in the top 40 of the 2016 NFL Draft, Whitehair would be the first offensive lineman from Kansas State to be drafted that high in the Super Bowl era.

Ideal Team Fit: With experience running zone and man blocking schemes at Kansas State, Whitehair has a scheme-diverse skill-set to fit any offense and start at guard or center as an NFL rookie.

NFL Comparison: A less gifted Zack Martin

Hoping to play at Kansas State one day, Cody Whitehair not only played for the Wildcats, but he was a core member of the team the last four seasons, splitting time between right tackle and left guard as a redshirt freshman and sophomore. He moved to left tackle as a junior in 2014 and started every game there the past two seasons, earning second-team All–Big 12 honors his final three seasons in Manhattan.

STRENGTHS: Balanced set-up and sinks hips at the point of attack. Quick off the snap with the wide base and shuffle to handle speed. Works hard to square, stick, and anchor while holding form with proper knee bend. At his best when he gets into rushers to make first contact and control their chest with a quick punch. Strong upper body to ride defenders away from the pocket. Athletic puller and controlled in space to connect and seal on second-level blocks. Veteran awareness with excellent vision and pressure instincts, keeping his head on a swivel. Tough as nails and plays through pain. Four-year starter with versatile experience at left tackle (26 starts), left guard (22), and right tackle (three), earning All–Big 12 honors all four seasons. Well-coached and considered the hardest worker on the team, leading by example.

WEAKNESSES: Short arms and limited growth potential. Bad habit of lunging due to his lack of length. Too much of a catch blocker and needs to be more aggressive with his hands to keep rushers from attacking his body, getting him upright and pushing him on his heels. Struggles to control the point of attack in the run game, relying on body position more than power in the run game. Needs to better control his momentum on the move and break down in space. Needs to eliminate the holding penalties with a bad habit of grabbing a fistful of jersey. Room to show more of a nasty attitude to bully, bury, and finish.

SUMMARY: A four-year starter, Whitehair says he prefers to play guard, but has extensive experience at tackle and practiced at center, playing wherever he was needed with his team-first attitude. He left an indelible mark at Kansas State with his leadership, work ethic, and high level of play the last four seasons, and boasts the professional make-up that will be welcomed in NFL locker rooms. Whitehair is assignment sound and rarely makes mistakes with the quick punch and shuffle to stone rushers in pass protection, but he isn't as effective on the move and needs to develop a more physical mean streak. He lacks the length to hold up consistently on the edges in the NFL, but Whitehair has the base strength, toughness, and instincts to be a long-term starter at either guard or center.

CAREER STATS

SEASON	GP/GS	POS
2012	13/12	9 LG, 3 RT
2013	13/13	13 LG
2014	13/13	13 LT
2015	13/13	LT
Career	52/51	26 LT, 22 LG, 3 RT

He left an indelible mark at Kansas State with his leadership, work ethic, and high level of play the last four seasons."

#20 PROSPECT
#1 OG

COMBINE RESULTS

GRADE	1ˢᵗ–2ⁿᵈ RD							
MEASURABLES	Arm: 32	Hand: 10 1/8	Wingspan: 79					
COMBINE	40-YD: 5.02	10-YD: 1.73	20-YD: 2.95	BP: 16	VJ: 25 1/2	BJ: 9'2"	SS: 4.58	3C: 7.32

DT / OLE MISS

Name: Robert Nkemdiche

Ht: 6′3½″ **Wt:** 294

Hometown/High School: Loganville, GA / Grayson

Class: Junior

Number: 5

DOB: September 19, 1994

Career Highlights: All-American (2015), All-American (2014), Freshman All-American (2013), Freshman All-SEC (2013)

Did You Know? If Nkemdiche joins Laremy Tunsil and Laquon Treadwell in round one, it would mark the first time Ole Miss produced three first-rounders in the same year.

Fun Fact: Originally committed to Clemson (along with his high school teammate Wayne Gallman), but changed his mind and joined his older brother at Ole Miss.

Ideal Team Fit: An explosive interior presence, Nkemdiche is a one-gap penetrator with All-Pro potential, but requires a defensive coach able to hone his talents like Rod Marinelli in Dallas.

NFL Comparison: Michael Bennett

Robert Nkemdiche (kim-DEE-chee) was lauded as the consensus top recruit out of high school, and though he never quite lived up to that billing on a consistent basis at Ole Miss, he showed flashes of dominance with an athletic and powerful skill-set for his size. Nkemdiche started 10 games as a true freshman and finished with 29 tackles, seven tackles for loss and three sacks, earning Freshman All-America and All-SEC honors. Nkemdiche started all 13 games in 2014 as a sophomore, recording 35 tackles, four tackles for loss, and two sacks to earn All-America honors. He finished 2015 with 34 tackles, eight tackles for loss, and two sacks as a junior.

STRENGTHS: Trimmed, well-conditioned body type with broad shoulders and a muscular frame. Balanced athlete with excellent flexibility and bend. Explosive off the ball to launch himself with cat-like quickness and a fast trigger. Lateral agility to skillfully cross the face of blockers, using his hip action to sink and redirect without losing momentum to his target. Very good in pursuit, playing with range and closing burst. Strong, aggressive hands to extend, punch, and drive, forcing blockers backward into the pocket. Plays low to the ground to beat blockers with leverage. Naturally powerful and has room to get even stronger. Versatile skill-set with experience inside and outside on the D-line. Also saw snaps on offense and special teams at Ole Miss with one receiving touchdown.

WEAKNESSES: Tends to play too fast and out of control, hindering his ability to break down in tight areas. Bad habit of turning his body once engaged to lean into blockers instead of consistently anchoring or using his hands. Gap integrity and on-field discipline need improvement, selling out and losing sight of the ball. Unimpressive career production with only 19 tackles for loss and seven sacks, disappearing for stretches during games. Inconsistent responses from hard coaching—does he want to be great? Off-field decision-making and accountability require investigation following multiple run-ins with the law.

SUMMARY: A three-year starter, Nkemdiche split his playing time between defensive end and defensive tackle for the Rebels and fits several positions at the next level. Nkemdiche has above-average athleticism and uses his movement skills and lower-body fluidity to skirt blockers and easily change directions. Although he sees plenty of double-teams and affects the game far more than what the box score says, his lack of production is a concern with only seven sacks in 34 career starts. Nkemdiche has explosive qualities for the position, but he is still learning the game and needs to develop his discipline and reliability both on and off the field. A high-risk/high-reward prospect, Nkemdiche isn't one of the top 10 football players in this draft, but he is one of the top 10 talents because of his remarkable traits.

CAREER STATS

SEASON	GP/GS	TACKLES	TFL	SACKS	FF
2013	11/10	29	7.0	3.0	0
2014	13/13	35	4.0	2.0	0
2015	11/11	34	8.0	2.0	0
Career	35/34	98	19.0	7.0	0

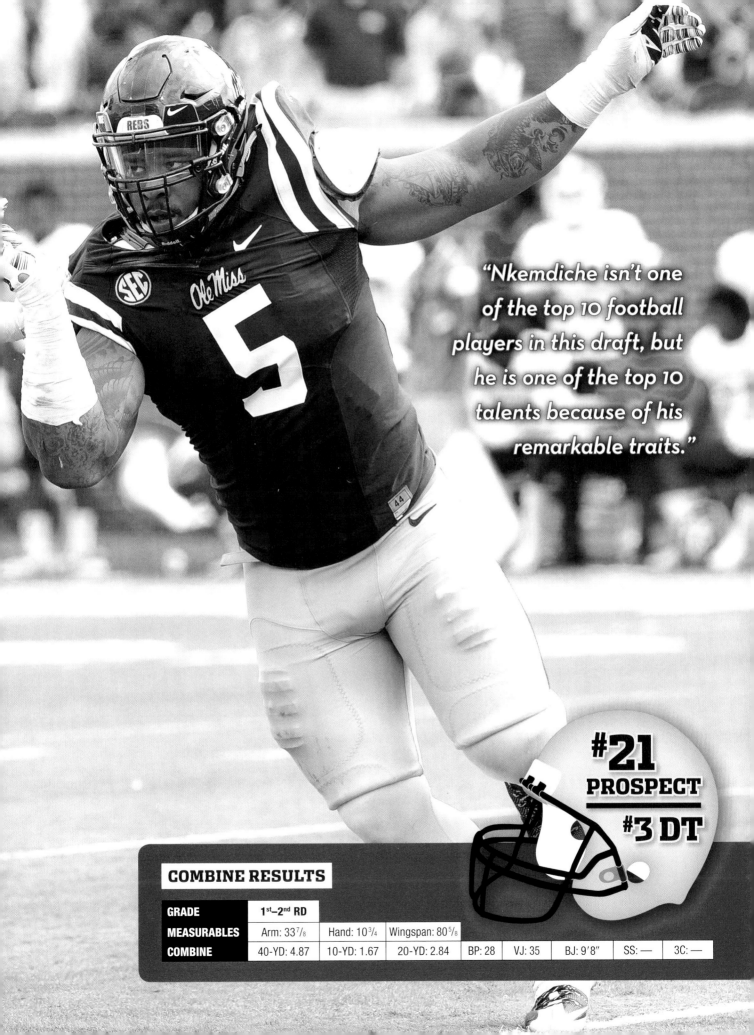

"Nkemdiche isn't one of the top 10 football players in this draft, but he is one of the top 10 talents because of his remarkable traits."

#21 PROSPECT
#3 DT

COMBINE RESULTS

GRADE	1ˢᵗ–2ⁿᵈ RD							
MEASURABLES	Arm: 33⁷/₈	Hand: 10³/₄	Wingspan: 80⁵/₈					
COMBINE	40-YD: 4.87	10-YD: 1.67	20-YD: 2.84	BP: 28	VJ: 35	BJ: 9'8"	SS: —	3C: —

ELI APPLE
CB / OHIO STATE

Name: Eli Apple

Ht: 6′⅝″ **Wt:** 199

Hometown/High School: Voorhees, NJ / Eastern

Class: Redshirt Sophomore

Number: 13

DOB: September 9, 1995

Career Highlights: Second-Team All–Big Ten (2015), CFP National Champion (2015)

Did You Know? When he arrived in Columbus, Apple struggled with continual fatigue during practice and was diagnosed with an iron deficiency that now requires daily medication.

Fun Fact: Changed his last name from "Woodard" to "Apple" his senior year in high school, taking the last name of his stepfather, who raised him.

Ideal Team Fit: A physical and good-sized athlete, Apple has the requisite traits to develop into an NFL team's No. 1 corner-back, projecting best in press and off-man schemes.

NFL Comparison: Bashaud Breeland

As the son of parents who work in television, Eli Apple is a well-traveled young man. He was born in Philadelphia, spent several years growing up in Ghana (his mother's birthplace), and then returned to the U.S., where he had stops in several states. Apple developed a close relationship with Jim Tressel in middle school and considered Ohio State his dream school, committing to the Buckeyes and redshirting in 2013. He earned a starting job as a redshirt freshman in 2014 and finished second on the team in passes defended (13), adding three interceptions. Apple started all 13 games as sophomore in 2015 and again finished second on the team with eight passes defended.

STRENGTHS: Tall, athletic frame with long arms and solid build. Coordinated athlete to bracket receivers downfield and consistently stay in phase. Controlled hop and footwork in his transition, using clean hip motion to mirror in man coverage. Disruptive and uses his length to keep receivers uncomfortable. Highly aggressive at the catch point with a "my ball" mentality. Competitive and not shy to take on blocks or throw his body around as a run defender. Physical once engaged to shed blockers on the perimeter. Improved route anticipation and field/sideline leverage while in man coverage. Tough-minded with a short memory. Battle-tested with 22 passes defended and four interceptions.

WEAKNESSES: Too hands-on downfield and lacks savvy at the top of routes. Target for penalties due to undisciplined hand placement, grabbing too much cloth. Experienced in press coverage at the line of scrimmage, but needs to improve his balance and jam technique. Tends to open his hips too early and struggles to recognize routes from bail position, creating sizeable cushions and allowing too many comeback completions. Plays too fast in pursuit, leading to overaggressive angles and missed tackles. Needs to improve his feel for the ball when back is to the line of scrimmage, struggling with timing. Required hard coaching when he arrived in Columbus.

SUMMARY: A two-year starter at cornerback, Apple earned a starting role as a redshirt freshman and held his own the last two seasons, playing both man and zone coverages. He possesses several traits for the cornerback position that translate well to the next level with his size, length, and athleticism. Apple isn't afraid to be physical and contest at the top of routes, but he's still learning what he can get away with and what will draw flags—desired length for the position, but NFL teams will be forced to live and die with his hands-on contact while he figures it out. Apple, who won't turn 21 years old until the start of the 2016 NFL season, is still very young, and with that comes on-field discipline issues, but he consistently stays in phase in press or off-man coverage and has appealing upside to be an impact NFL starter.

CAREER STATS

SEASON	GP/GS	TACKLES	TFL	SACKS	FF	PASS DEF	INT
2013	Redshirted						
2014	15/14	53	5.5	0.0	1	13	3
2015	13/13	33	2.0	0.0	0	9	1
Career	28/27	86	7.5	0.0	1	22	4

"He possesses several traits for the cornerback position that translate well to the next level with his size, length, and athleticism."

#22
PROSPECT

#3 CB

COMBINE RESULTS

GRADE	1st–2nd RD							
MEASURABLES	Arm: 31⅜	Hand: 9⅜	Wingspan: 76⅜					
COMBINE	40-YD: 4.40	10-YD: 1.53	20-YD: 2.59	BP: 13	VJ: —	BJ: —	SS: —	3C: —

A'SHAWN ROBINSON
DT / ALABAMA

Name: A'Shawn Robinson

Ht: 6'3⅝" **Wt:** 307

Hometown/High School: Fort Worth, TX / Arlington Heights

Class: Junior

Number: 86

DOB: March 21, 1995

Career Highlights: CFP National Champion (2016), First-Team All-SEC (2015), Freshman All-American (2013)

Did You Know? Didn't apply for feedback from the NFL Draft Advisory Committee, instead relied on the advice of Nick Saban and his NFL contacts who told him he would be a first-round pick.

Fun Fact: Nicknamed the "man child" by his mother growing up because she literally had to keep his birth certificate in her purse to prove her son was playing in the appropriate age group.

Ideal Team Fit: A three-down defender who fits even or odd fronts, Robinson is still young and needs fine-tuning in areas, but he will start early in his career due to his versatility to play in any scheme.

NFL Comparison: Michael Brockers

A five-star defensive tackle recruit out of high school, A'Shawn Robinson was one of the top prep players in Texas and initially ver-balled to the Longhorns as a junior before switching his commitment to Alabama before signing day. He saw immediate action as a true freshman before becoming a full-time starter in 2014 as a sophomore, recording 49 tackles and 6.5 tackles for loss, splitting his time between nose tackle and five-technique spots. He started all 15 games as a junior in 2015, finishing with 46 tackles, 7.5 tackles for loss, and 3.5 sacks to earn first-team All-SEC honors.

STRENGTHS: Big-boned frame with proportionate thickness throughout—a physically mature, grown man. Powerful core and limbs to control the point of attack and stack-and-shed. Smooth athleticism with the lateral range to mirror and scrape down the line of scrimmage in pursuit. Hip flexibility and body control to work tight spaces. Shows the ability to lock out, press the hole, and make stops in the gap. Plays with shock in his hands to work through the trash. Can sink and drive his lower body to create separation from blocks or push the pocket. Strong ball awareness and backfield vision to recognize things quickly. Uses his big hands and long arms to knock the ball down at the line of scrimmage (five passes defended and three blocked kicks in his career). Draws constant double-teams to keep blockers busy. Well-versed in multiple D-line techniques. Responds well to coaching and applies what he learns during the week. Humble, low-key personality and dedicated in the classroom.

WEAKNESSES: Underwhelming initial move and allows his pads to rise at contact, playing too upright and losing leverage. Doesn't play with natural explosiveness, more of a one-note chaser. Below-average pass-rush skill-set, lacking the hand sequence or burst to consistently penetrate the pocket. Thinks too much, causing him to be a step late. Needs to be more disciplined stacking the edge to hold outside contain and gain body angles. Wears himself out and just goes through the motions on some snaps. Unimpressive career production.

SUMMARY: A two-year starter in Alabama's 3-4 base defense, Robinson lined up everywhere from the zero- to six-technique positions on the right side of the defensive line, showing the ability control multiple gaps as a five-technique or anchor at nose tackle. A stout run defender, Robinson is raw as a pass rusher, but his production doesn't always show on the stat sheet—was mostly asked to two-gap, clog things up, and occupy blockers to free up the linebackers at Alabama. He tends to tire easily and is a frustrating player on tape because his flashes are very good, but they don't happen consistently. Robinson is the poster prospect for the golden rule of scouting ("traits over production"), and his traits have NFL scouts drooling.

CAREER STATS

SEASON	GP/GS	TACKLES	TFL	SACKS	FF
2013	13/2	38	8.0	5.5	0
2014	14/13	49	6.5	0.0	1
2015	15/15	46	7.5	3.5	0
Career	42/30	133	22.0	9.0	1

"Robinson is the poster prospect for the golden rule of scouting ('traits over production'), and his traits have NFL scouts drooling."

#23 PROSPECT

#4 DT

COMBINE RESULTS

GRADE	1ˢᵗ–2ⁿᵈ RD							
MEASURABLES	Arm: 34½	Hand: 10½	Wingspan: 83½					
COMBINE	40-YD: 5.20	10-YD: 1.78	20-YD: 3.01	BP: 22	VJ: 26	BJ: 8'10"	SS: 4.74	3C: 7.80

TAYLOR DECKER
OT / OHIO STATE

Name: Taylor Decker

Ht: 6'7" **Wt:** 310

Hometown/High School: Vandalia, OH / Butler

Class: Senior

Number: 68

DOB: August 23, 1994

Career Highlights: Rimington-Pace Big Ten Offensive Lineman of the Year (2015), All-American (2015), First-Team All–Big Ten (2015), CFP National Champion (2015), Second-Team All–Big Ten (2014)

Did You Know? Originally committed to Notre Dame, but received an offer from Ohio State (his "dream school") once Urban Meyer was hired, switching his commitment to the Buckeyes.

Fun Fact: A lover of animals, Decker earned his degree in animal sciences from Ohio State and interned the past two years at the Columbus Zoo, caring for animals and giving tours.

Ideal Team Fit: Although he doesn't have a high ceiling, Decker is NFL-ready right now and will compete for immediate snaps as a rookie at either guard or right tackle.

NFL Comparison: Quicker version of Jack Mewhort

A two-sport stand-out in high school who received interest from mid-majors to play college basketball, Taylor Decker earned the starting right tackle job at Ohio State as a sophomore. He had a rough debut against Buffalo's Khalil Mack (a top-five pick of the Oakland Raiders in the 2014 NFL Draft) in his first career start but has been an ascending talent since. Decker moved over to left tackle as a junior in 2014 and started all 15 games for the national champion Buckeyes, earning second-team All–Big Ten honors. He returned for his senior season and again started every game at left tackle, earning the Rimington-Pace Big Ten Offensive Lineman of the Year award.

STRENGTHS: Physically mature with a large frame, essential body girth, and very good core strength. Utilizes his reach and strong hands to latch-and-control rushers from the outset. Despite his height, shows the natural knee bend and sturdy anchor to absorb the rush and reestablish his base. Has the power and punch to neutralize speed. Balanced in his movements and shifts his weight well to shuffle and recover. Terrific timing at the second level with the mobility to pull and occupy linebackers in space. Physical drive blocker and plays with the nasty streak and competitive demeanor needed for the next level. Reliable, well-spoken, and vocal leader with the makeup to start from day one in the NFL. All-America résumé with durable experience as a three-year starter—first Buckeyes tackle to earn Big Ten Offensive Lineman of the Year since Orlando Pace.

WEAKNESSES: Naturally tall pad level and will lose the leverage battle when rushers are able to get underneath him. Has the knee bend to sink and absorb, but can be late to drop his hips, taking away his anchor strength. Needs to be more technically proficient with his reach and hand placement mid-kick-slide. Inconsistent snap anticipation and can be late to set up—has reps on film where he seems to fall asleep, missing his usual urgency. Has the aggressive take-on strength to sustain blocks, but needs to better use angles to his advantage. Still developing his pre-snap recognition skills and can be fooled by delayed pressures.

SUMMARY: A three-year starter, Decker started the last 42 games at Ohio State, splitting time between left and right tackle, and was part of a Buckeyes' senior class that won 50 games. He has the reliable character, can-do attitude, and pro-ready make-up that fits NFL locker rooms (would be in the military if not for football). He can struggle at times with speed off the edge, especially flexible rushers who can bend underneath him, but Decker has the frame, balance, and forceful hands to neutralize quickness and control the point of attack.

CAREER STATS

SEASON	GP/GS	POS
2012	12/0	*Special Teams*
2013	14/14	RT
2014	15/15	LT
2015	13/13	LT
Career	54/42	28 LT, 14 RT

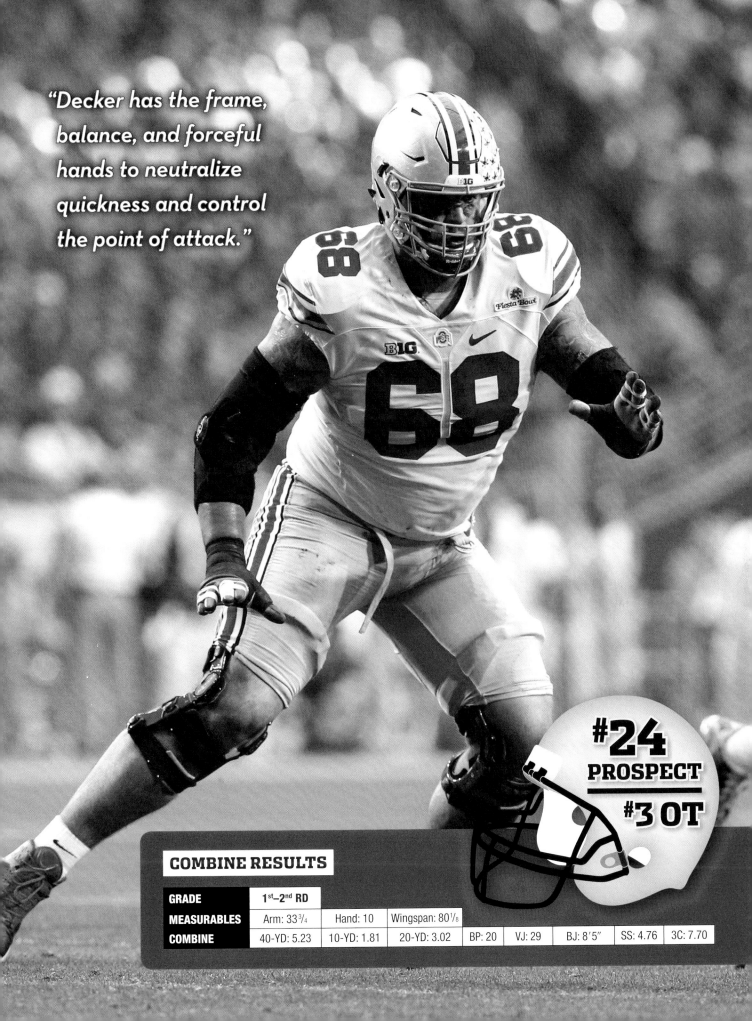

"Decker has the frame, balance, and forceful hands to neutralize quickness and control the point of attack."

#24 PROSPECT
#3 OT

COMBINE RESULTS

GRADE	1st–2nd RD							
MEASURABLES	Arm: 33¾	Hand: 10	Wingspan: 80⅛					
COMBINE	40-YD: 5.23	10-YD: 1.81	20-YD: 3.02	BP: 20	VJ: 29	BJ: 8'5"	SS: 4.76	3C: 7.70

COREY COLEMAN
WR / BAYLOR

Name: Corey Coleman

Ht: 5'10⅝" **Wt:** 194

Hometown/High School: Richardson, TX / Pearce

Class: Redshirt Junior

Number: 1

DOB: July 6, 1994

Career Highlights: Unanimous All-American (2015), Biletnikoff Award (2015), First-Team All–Big 12 (2015), Second-Team All–Big 12 (2014)

Did You Know? Set new school records for touchdown catches in a single season (20) and career (33), finishing in the top five in Baylor history in receiving yards (3,009) and 100-yard performances (12).

Fun Fact: Groomed by his godfather and 14-year NFL veteran Ray Crockett, who was a role model and father figure throughout Coleman's youth.

Ideal Team Fit: Requires a patient coaching staff because he will need time to adjust to the NFL game, but once he does, look out. He will fit well with a team that frequently attacks every level of the defense through the air like the Baltimore Ravens or New Orleans Saints.

NFL Comparison: Emmanuel Sanders

With 20 touchdown catches through the first eight games of 2015, Corey Coleman put his name on the national radar as a legitimate Heisman Trophy contender and one of the most talented wideouts in the country. His production tailed off in the final month of the season due to injuries at the quarterback position, but he became the first Baylor player to win the Biletnikoff Award and the ninth in school history to earn unanimous All-America honors. Coleman connected with Baylor early in the recruiting process, and the Bears were one of the few teams that wanted him at receiver instead of cornerback.

STRENGTHS: Shredded muscle tone and developed physique. Plays with deceiving body strength to keep his feet through contact and fight for extra yardage. Explosive athlete with quick shake off the line of scrimmage to beat the jam and at the top of routes to create spacing. Springs in his calves to juke out of trouble or elevate to make plays above the rim, not allowing contested situations to bother him. Needs only one step to accelerate up to full speed, stack the corner, and hit a fifth gear to finish. Shows excellent tracking skills downfield with natural body control to make himself available in his routes. Quick, strong hands and attacks the ball before it can reach his body. Physically tough, and it's not easy to knock him off his route. Passionate, strong-willed competitor who hates to lose.

WEAKNESSES: Lacks ideal height or length for the position, and his frame appears near maxed out under 200 pounds. Will have his share of drops, running before securing or not finishing to the ground. Wasn't asked to run a full route tree with most of his production coming on screens and go routes. Faced mostly soft cushions in the Big 12, rarely facing press or any type of physical presence on the outside. Normally doesn't allow his lack of size to limit him, but he will hear footsteps over the middle at times and play with T-rex arms. Feisty, but largely unproven as a blocker. Will lose his composure on the field at times and is still learning how to properly control his intense demeanor.

SUMMARY: A three-year starter, Coleman starred in Art Briles' wide-open spread offense, which is mostly half-field reads and unchallenged routes, making it difficult to compare his college film to what he'll see in the NFL. Despite average height/length, Coleman is deceptively powerful with explosive athleticism and strong balance to be a threat at all levels of the field. He plays bigger than he looks with above-average hand-eye coordination to attack the ball away from his body. Although his pro evaluation requires a leap of faith due to Baylor's offense, Coleman has the athletic traits and competitive temperament that suggest it's only a matter of time before he finds NFL success.

CAREER STATS

SEASON	GP/GS	REC	REC YD	REC AVG	REC TD
2012	Redshirted				
2013	13/10	35	527	15.1	2
2014	10/6	64	1,119	17.5	11
2015	12/12	74	1,363	18.4	20
Career	35/28	173	3,009	17.4	33

"Coleman has the athletic traits and competitive temperament that suggest it's only a matter of time before he finds NFL success."

#25 PROSPECT

#2 WR

COMBINE RESULTS

GRADE	1st–2nd RD							
MEASURABLES	Arm: 30¼	Hand: 9	Wingspan: 72⅞					
COMBINE	40-YD: —	10-YD: —	20-YD: —	BP: 17	VJ: 40½	BJ: 10′9″	SS: —	3C: —

PAXTON LYNCH
QB / MEMPHIS

Name: Paxton Lynch

Ht: 6′6⅝″ **Wt:** 244

Hometown/High School: Deltona, FL / Trinity Christian Academy

Class: Redshirt Junior

Number: 12

DOB: February 12, 1994

Career Highlights: First-Team All-AAC (2015), Second-Team All-AAC (2014)

Did You Know? Won 19 games as a starter the past two seasons, including the program's first 10-win season since the 1930s, leaving Memphis with a 22–16 career record as a starter.

Fun Fact: Thought he was headed to Florida to play for the Gators, but once offensive coordinator Charlie Weis took the head coaching job at Kansas, the offer never arrived. Florida gave the spot to Skyler Mornhinweg instead, asking Lynch to walk on.

Ideal Team Fit: A prospect who has been mostly self-taught at the position, Lynch requires a patient support system in the NFL and a situation where he can sit and learn before thrown into action, similar to Brock Osweiler in Denver.

NFL Comparison: Mix of Brock Osweiler and Colin Kaepernick

Still very young in quarterback years, Paxton Lynch showed impressive development over the last three seasons at Memphis and boasts the upside that has NFL teams intrigued. Due to his high school running a wing-T offense, Lynch was vastly overlooked as a recruit with only two scholarship offers (Florida A&M and Memphis). After an inconsistent freshman season, Lynch showed significant strides as a sophomore with 35 total TDs (22 passing/13 rushing), leading Memphis to 10 wins and a conference title. He improved his production as a junior, completing 66.8% of passes and setting single-season school records in passing yards (3,778) and TDs (28) in 2015.

STRENGTHS: Tall, lanky frame with broad shoulders and the build to take a beating in the NFL. Light on his feet with the athleticism and body control to climb, shuffle, and slide in the pocket, buying time and adjusting his throwing platform. Throws with accuracy on the move. Arm strength to fire strikes with a quick trigger. Longer arms, but easily loads and delivers in a clean motion. Quick eyes to scan and make whole-field reads. Improved poise to sense pressure and is comfortable operating in a tight pocket. Recognizes the blitz and knows his hot routes. Has the arm to get away with throwing without a firm base. Improved placement, especially on slants and in-breaking routes, to put the ball where only his man can get it. Picks up things quickly, and coaches talk highly of his ability to learn and apply. Unforced team mentality. Genuinely enjoys playing football, but loves the camaraderie of his teammates even more.

WEAKNESSES: Inconsistent footwork. Doesn't always throw with a balanced platform, which affects his downfield accuracy, relying on arm talent more than fundamentals. Requires maintenance with his throwing technique, something that's probably never been stressed by his coaches. Internal clock is still a work-in-progress, taking sacks that he shouldn't. Sound decision maker, but still learning which throws he should and shouldn't make. Needs work on his touch and timing. All the calls in the Memphis offense came from the sideline. Confident player, but not overly vocal and still developing his leadership style.

SUMMARY: A three-year starter, Lynch has some experience under center, but spent most of his time in the shotgun in Memphis' movement spread offense, which implemented a lot of play-action and option plays. A late bloomer, Lynch is just a "kid playing a game" right now, according to his coaches, and is largely self-taught at the position. From a scouting perspective, Lynch needs mechanical work and on-field reps, but he checks boxes for his size, athleticism, arm talent, field vision, and appetite for football. His pro transition will require time, and although he might not be "perfect" in every area, the ingredients are there for Lynch to develop into an NFL starter.

CAREER STATS

SEASON	GP/GS	CMP	ATT	PCT	YDS	TDS	INT
2012				Redshirted			
2013	12/12	203	349	58.2	2,056	9	10
2014	13/13	259	413	62.7	3,031	22	9
2015	13/13	296	443	66.8	3,778	28	4
Career	38/38	758	1,205	62.9	8,865	59	23

"Lynch needs mechanical work and on-field reps, but he checks boxes for his size, athleticism, arm talent, field vision, and appetite for football."

#26 PROSPECT

#3 QB

COMBINE RESULTS

GRADE	1ˢᵗ–2ⁿᵈ RD							
MEASURABLES	Arm: 34¼	Hand: 10¼	Wingspan: 81¾					
COMBINE	40-YD: 4.86	10-YD: 1.69	20-YD: 2.81	BP: —	VJ: 36	BJ: 9'10"	SS: 4.26	3C: 7.14

ANDREW BILLINGS
DT / BAYLOR

Name: Andrew Billings

Ht: 6′5⅝″ **Wt:** 311

Hometown/High School: Waco, TX / Waco

Class: Junior

Number: 75

DOB: March 6, 1995

Career Highlights: First-Team All–Big 12 (2015), Big 12 Defensive Player of the Year (2015), Big 12 Defensive Lineman of the Year (2015), First-Team All–Big 12 (2014)

Did You Know? Became the first player in school history to earn Big 12 Defensive Player of the Year honors.

Fun Fact: Broke two-time Olympian and former WWE wrestler Mark Henry's 1990 Texas prep state record with 2,010-pound effort (805 squat, 500 bench, 705 dead lift).

Ideal Team Fit: Built low to the ground with a powerful base, Billings projects as a versatile interior player with the skill-set to fit the zero- or one-techniques in even and odd fronts.

NFL Comparison: Bennie Logan

Raised in Baylor's backyard, Andrew Billings looked forward to leaving Waco for college, even committing to TCU at one point. But ultimately, he decided that his hometown program was his best fit, both athletically and academically. He saw his playing time increase throughout the 2013 season as a true freshman, finishing with 30 tackles and four tackles for loss. He was the starting nose tackle in every game as a sophomore and recorded 37 tackles, 11.5 tackles for loss, and two sacks, earning first-team All–Big 12 honors. Billings started 12 games as a junior in 2015 and led the team with 15 tackles for loss and 5.5 sacks, adding a career-best 40 tackles to earn first-team All–Big 12 honors. He was also named the 2015 Big 12 Defensive Player and Defensive Lineman of the Year.

STRENGTHS: Built low to the ground with a thick bubble to stay balanced through contact. Strong as an ox with core power and natural leverage. Understands point-of-attack maneuvers with strong hands to rip, pull, and control blockers. Lower-body flexibility to plant and burst out of his stance and play quick off the ball. Athletic on his feet to avoid cut blocks and smoothly scrape around the trash. Plays with force, locking out and driving his legs to move bodies. Endures, won't wear down. Loves the weight room and his first love was powerlifting. Toughs out injuries with a resilient attitude. Productive, leading the team in tackles for loss and sacks in 2015.

WEAKNESSES: Shorter than ideal with only average arm length. Stiff midsection and doesn't consistently explode through his hips. Relies on forward lean, leading to snaps where he overextends and ends up on the ground. Limited lateral range to shuffle up and down the line of scrimmage. Underdeveloped instincts and tends to think too much, causing him to be late to locate. Room to improve his pre-snap recognition and mechanics. Marginal pass-rush savvy. Minor durability concerns due to a nagging left leg injury (October 2015).

SUMMARY: A two-year starter in Baylor's multiple defensive front, Billings lined up mostly as the nose tackle or one-technique over the A-gap. He was powerful versus the run, clogging the middle and opening tackle lanes for his teammates, and also disrupted the backfield with 30.5 tackles for loss in 27 career starts. He focused on weight-lifting since seventh grade and played mostly offensive line in high school, so he's still learning how good he can be as an interior defensive lineman. Although he needs to improve his backfield vision and ball awareness, Billings flashes dominant qualities when he keeps his pad level low, rolls his hips at the point of attack, and pushes his momentum into the pocket. As the technique and discipline catch up to his brawling strength and revving motor, Billings will continue to get better.

CAREER STATS

SEASON	GP/GS	TACKLES	TFL	SACKS	FF
2013	11/2	30	4.0	0.5	0
2014	13/13	37	11.5	2.0	1
2015	12/12	40	15.0	5.5	1
Career	36/27	107	30.5	8.0	2

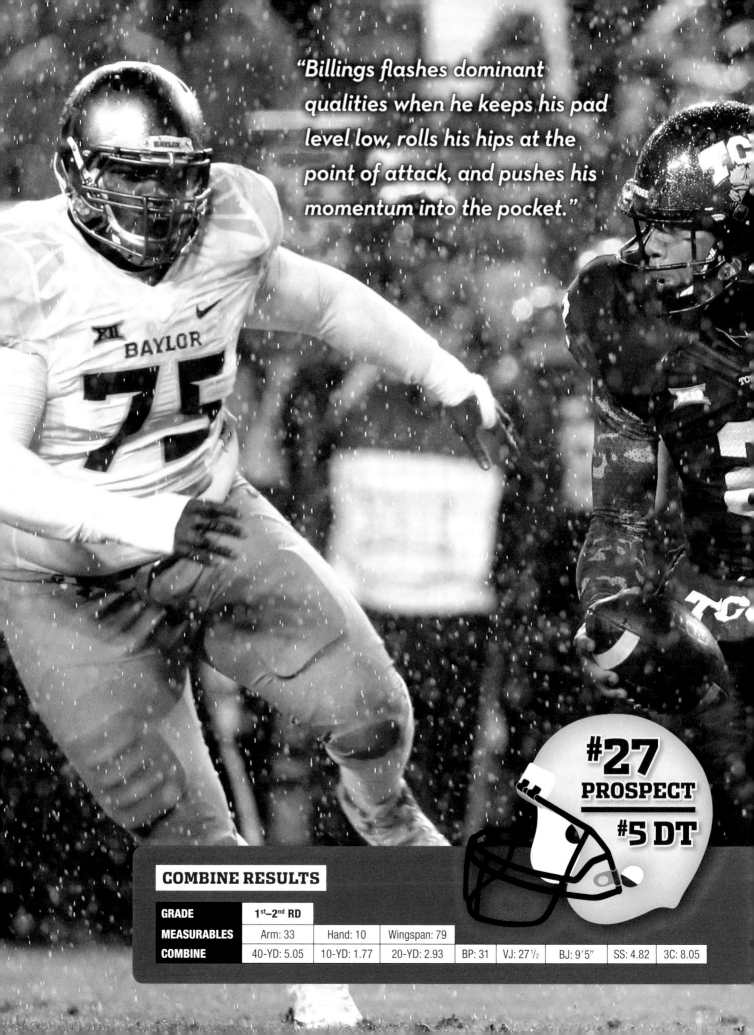

"Billings flashes dominant qualities when he keeps his pad level low, rolls his hips at the point of attack, and pushes his momentum into the pocket."

#27 PROSPECT

#5 DT

COMBINE RESULTS

GRADE	1ˢᵗ–2ⁿᵈ RD							
MEASURABLES	Arm: 33	Hand: 10	Wingspan: 79					
COMBINE	40-YD: 5.05	10-YD: 1.77	20-YD: 2.93	BP: 31	VJ: 27½	BJ: 9'5"	SS: 4.82	3C: 8.05

VERNON BUTLER
DT / LOUISIANA TECH

Name: Vernon Butler

Ht: 6'3⅝" **Wt:** 323

Hometown/High School: Summit, MS / North Pike

Class: Senior

Number: 9

DOB: June 14, 1994

Career Highlights: Senior Bowl (2016), First-Team All–Conference USA (2015), Honorable Mention All–Conference USA (2014)

Did You Know? If drafted in round one, Butler would be the first defensive player from Louisiana Tech to hear his name called in the draft's top 32 selections.

Fun Fact: Butler held scholarship offers from several SEC programs like Ole Miss and Mississippi State, but he fell in love with Louisiana Tech.

Ideal Team Fit: The beauty to Butler is his versatile skill-set that will entice all 32 NFL teams. He can play multiple techniques in either 3-4 or 4-3 schemes.

NFL Comparison: Linval Joseph

"Big Vern" Butler received attention from several SEC programs out of high school, but he chose to play his college ball for the Bulldogs. He was a backup as a true freshman and sophomore, but saw his snaps increase each game and earned his first start in 2013. With Justin Ellis off to the NFL (107th overall to the Oakland Raiders in 2014 draft), Butler became a full-time starter as a junior and recorded a career-best 56 tackles and 13.5 tackles for loss. He returned for his senior season in 2015 and earned first-team All–Conference USA honors with 50 tackles, 10 tackles for loss, and a career-best three sacks.

STRENGTHS: Wide, powerful hips and carries his weight well. Short-area quickness and lateral range to work up and down the line of scrimmage and sidestep blocks. Strong upper body to create movement off the snap, using his balance and length to extend into blocks and convert initial step to power. Coordinated movements to work off contact and stay within striking distance. Sees through blockers with improved tracking awareness. Excellent pursuit speed and playing range for his size. Active hands and reach to stack the corner and work to get free. Hits behind his pads with closing surge. Plays with energy and shows the same intensity in the fourth quarter as the opening drive. Consistent competitor and senior captain with a strong football appetite. ("He loves the game of football," said Tech's QB Jeff Driskel.) Sturdy and battle-tested, starting every game the last two seasons.

WEAKNESSES: Plays too upright off the snap and relies on his upper-body power instead of using leverage and knee bend. Strong when squared, but struggles to control blocks when not nose-to-nose, limiting his ability to break free and make stops on ball carriers in the gap. Narrow-shouldered and needs to do a better job keeping blockers from his body, maintaining space to better create separation. Active hands and limbs, but needs to show more purpose and strategy behind his rush moves. Minimal sack production in college.

SUMMARY: Butler lined up all over Louisiana Tech's multiple front, spending most of his time at three- and five-technique spots and moving inside to nose tackle in passing situations. He flashes on tape with the lower-body athleticism and upper-body power to stack blockers and make stops at or behind the line of scrimmage (23.5 tackles for loss as a starter). Butler plays balanced on his feet with coordinated movements, but needs to improve his pad level to better clear single blockers when not squared up. Although he needs to develop his pass-rush technique, Butler will appeal to both even and odd fronts with his relentless playing temperament, lateral quickness, and power to control the point of attack.

CAREER STATS

SEASON	GP/GS	TACKLES	TFL	SACKS	FF
2012	11/0	21	1.5	0.0	0
2013	11/1	43	4.5	1.0	0
2014	14/14	56	13.5	1.0	1
2015	13/13	50	10.0	3.0	0
Career	49/28	170	29.5	5.0	1

"Butler flashes on tape with the lower-body athleticism and upper-body power to stack blockers and make stops at or behind the line of scrimmage."

#28 PROSPECT

#6 DT

COMBINE RESULTS

GRADE	1ˢᵗ–2ⁿᵈ RD							
MEASURABLES	Arm: 35	Hand: 10	Wingspan: 83⁷/₈					
COMBINE	40-YD: 5.33	10-YD: 1.82	20-YD: 3.07	BP: 26	VJ: 29½	BJ: 8'8"	SS: 4.76	3C: 7.82

JONATHAN BULLARD
DE / FLORIDA

Name: Jonathan Bullard

Ht: 6′3″ **Wt:** 285

Hometown/High School: Shelby, NC / Crest Senior

Class: Senior

Number: 90

DOB: October 22, 1993

Career Highlights: First-Team All-SEC (2015), Freshman All-SEC (2012)

Did You Know? If drafted in the first round, it would be the fourth straight season the Gators have produced a first-round defensive lineman (2015: Dante Fowler; 2014: Dominique Easley; 2013: Sharrif Floyd).

Fun Fact: Florida defensive coordinator Geoff Collins called Bullard the "poster child" for work ethic and character, handling the transition of a new coaching staff.

Ideal Team Fit: Bullard is scheme diverse as a prospect and can legitimately play anywhere from the three- to six-technique positions in the NFL, fitting even and odd fronts. His ideal fit is setting the edge as a defensive end before kicking inside as a penetrating three-technique on passing downs.

NFL Comparison: Jason Jones

Ranked as the No. 1 defensive line recruit out of high school, Jonathan Bullard signed with Florida to be the next top pass rusher for the Gators, but after seeing part-time action as a freshman and sophomore, he transitioned to a hybrid defensive tackle role. Although he made the move begrudgingly, Bullard benefited from seeing snaps inside and developing his versatility. After a productive junior year, many expected him to turn pro, but he chose to return to Gainesville for his senior year, boosting his draft stock in the process. Bullard set career-highs in 2015 and led Florida with 17.5 tackles for loss and 6.5 sacks, earning first-team All-SEC honors.

STRENGTHS: Well-built frame with long arms and a powerful upper body. Excellent snap anticipation to burst off the ball, extend into blockers, and create movement. Quick first step to swim and invade the backfield. Lateral agility to sidestep blocks and change directions. Instinctive and senses his surroundings quickly, reading the ball carrier or blocker and staying patient to break down. Locates the ball well and trusts his vision to track. Fierce hands and initial momentum to dislodge blockers and stack-shed with ferocity. Improved his pass-rush skills and understands how to break the rhythm of blockers. Experienced inside as a three-technique defensive tackle and outside at defensive end—can two-gap and play multiple techniques with his versatility. Never shuts it down and won't disappear from games, frequently playing through pain. Praised for his work ethic and character by the Florida coaching staff. Production improved each season, finishing third in the SEC in tackles for loss as a senior.

WEAKNESSES: High cut and plays with lower body stiffness, showing some tweener traits. Overaggressive downhill and doesn't consistently come to balance in pursuit. Bad habit of allowing his pads to rise once engaged, losing leverage and playing too high. Easily moved by double-teams and needs to better sink and anchor his lower body. Hand placement is improved, but not consistent. Needs to eliminate the penalties, especially the late hits. Plays through pain, but often banged up—medical reports will be important.

SUMMARY: A three-year starter, Bullard played all over the Florida defensive line throughout his career and can legitimately play anywhere from the three- to six-technique position in the NFL. Bullard is a certified tough guy who will play through pain and find ways to be disruptive, drawing praise from his coaches for his textbook football character. He is limited as a pass rusher, but shows fantastic reflexes and recognition at the point of attack to read, stack, and shed blockers, owning the tenacious competitive drive needed to be a wrecking ball at the line of scrimmage.

CAREER STATS

SEASON	GP/GS	TACKLES	TFL	SACKS	FF
2012	13/2	27	5.0	1.5	0
2013	11/8	33	2.5	1.5	0
2014	12/12	52	8.5	2.5	0
2015	14/14	66	17.5	6.5	0
Career	50/36	178	33.5	12.0	0

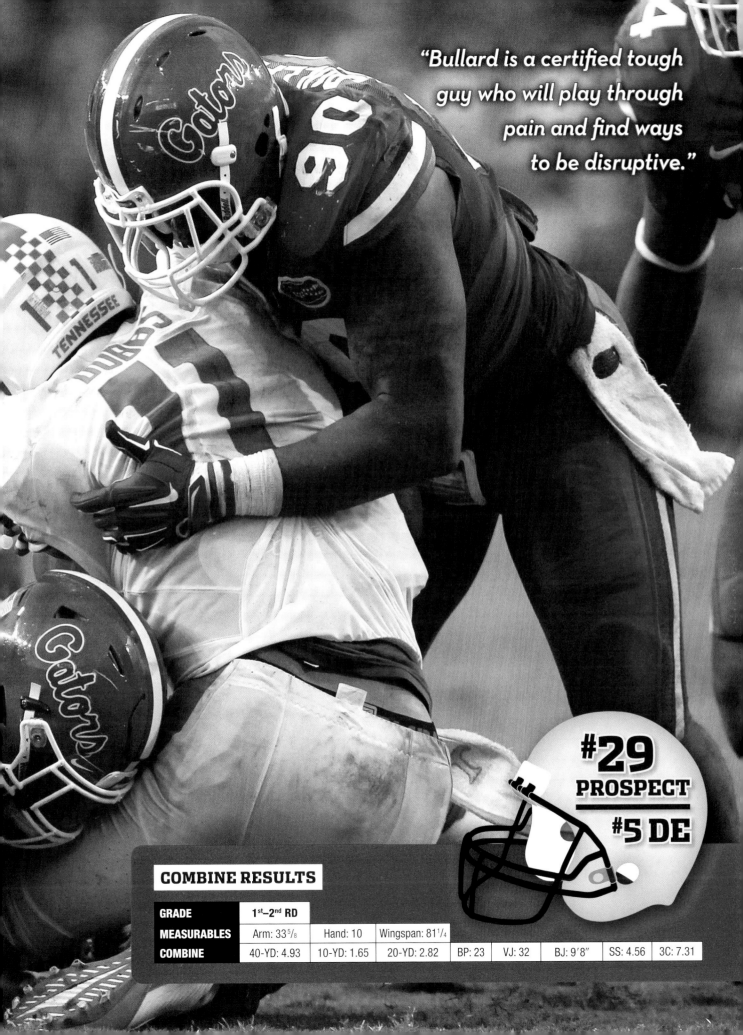

"Bullard is a certified tough guy who will play through pain and find ways to be disruptive."

#29 PROSPECT

#5 DE

COMBINE RESULTS

GRADE	1st–2nd RD							
MEASURABLES	Arm: 33⅝	Hand: 10	Wingspan: 81¼					
COMBINE	40-YD: 4.93	10-YD: 1.65	20-YD: 2.82	BP: 23	VJ: 32	BJ: 9'8"	SS: 4.56	3C: 7.31

KENNY CLARK
DT / UCLA

Name: Kenny Clark

Ht: 6′2⅝″ **Wt:** 314

Hometown/High School:
San Bernardino, CA / Carter

Class: Junior

Number: 97

DOB: October 4, 1995

Career Highlights: First-Team All-Pac-12 (2015), Second-Team All-Pac-12 (2014)

Did You Know? At only 20 years old, Clark is one of the youngest prospects in the 2016 class, not turning 21 years old until a few weeks into his rookie NFL season.

Fun Fact: Saw reps on offense in red-zone situations for the Bruins as both a lead blocker and tight end, hauling in a three-yard touchdown catch in the 2015 season opener versus Virginia.

Ideal Team Fit: While still developing as a pass rusher, Clark is a power-packed and stout run defender who should settle into a nose tackle role for a 4-3 scheme like the Cincinnati Bengals, initially as a two-down defender with potential to be more.

NFL Comparison: Domata Peko

A heavyweight champion wrestler in high school, Kenny Clark translates a lot of those techniques from the mat to the football field. He was wooed by every West Coast program as a recruit, committing to UCLA and working his way into the starting lineup as a true freshman. Clark started all 13 games as a sophomore in 2014, finishing with 58 tackles, 5.5 tackles for loss, and earning second-team All-Pac-12 honors. He again started all 13 games as a junior in 2015 and finished second on the team with 75 tackles, setting career highs in tackles for loss (11) and sacks (6) to earn first-team All-Pac-12 honors.

STRENGTHS: Plays with low hips, leverage, and several wrestling maneuvers. Flexible athlete with body control and redirection skills to pursue and break down in short spaces. Strong upper body with a powerful rip-and-club move to swat at the point of attack. Initial quickness off the snap to stack-and-shed initial blocks, drive his feet, and break through the line of scrimmage. Understands hand placement and works hard to gain inside positioning. Quick punch, shooting his reach to engage blockers. Balanced feet through congestion with range to make stops away from scrimmage. Quick to recognize screens and make plays in pursuit—impressive tackle total as a junior (75). Maintains technique through contact to generate movement and attract double-teams. Aggressive demeanor and determined individual. Excellent work habits and treats practice like a game—well-respected team captain.

WEAKNESSES: Lacks elite size and growth potential for the position with only average length. Tends to stop his feet at the point of attack, relying on his upper body to shed blocks, which leads to hand-fighting. Inconsistent locating skills with a bad habit of ducking his head at contact. Late to plays outside the hashes, lacking closing burst to finish. Moved from his spot and beat by angle blocks, cutting him off from run lanes. Struggles to string together moves as a pass rusher. Doesn't come off the field much, which will cause him to take plays off, loafing at times when the play isn't run at him.

SUMMARY: A two-year starter, Clark lined up primarily as a nose tackle and one-technique in UCLA's 4-3 base defense, often in a frog stance with both hands in the dirt. He is powerful at the point of attack to overwhelm blockers and reestablish the line of scrimmage, shutting down the middle of the field versus the run. Clark flashes the violence, agility, and motor to twist and drive blockers backward, but is still young physically and conceptually, and he will need to prove himself as an every-down defender once he arrives in an NFL camp. While unpolished in areas, Clark has the production that matches the tape due to his hustle, power, and mechanics.

CAREER STATS

SEASON	GP/GS	TACKLES	TFL	SACKS	FF
2013	13/4	31	4.0	1.0	1
2014	13/13	58	5.5	0.0	0
2015	13/13	75	11.0	6.0	0
Career	39/30	164	20.5	7.0	1

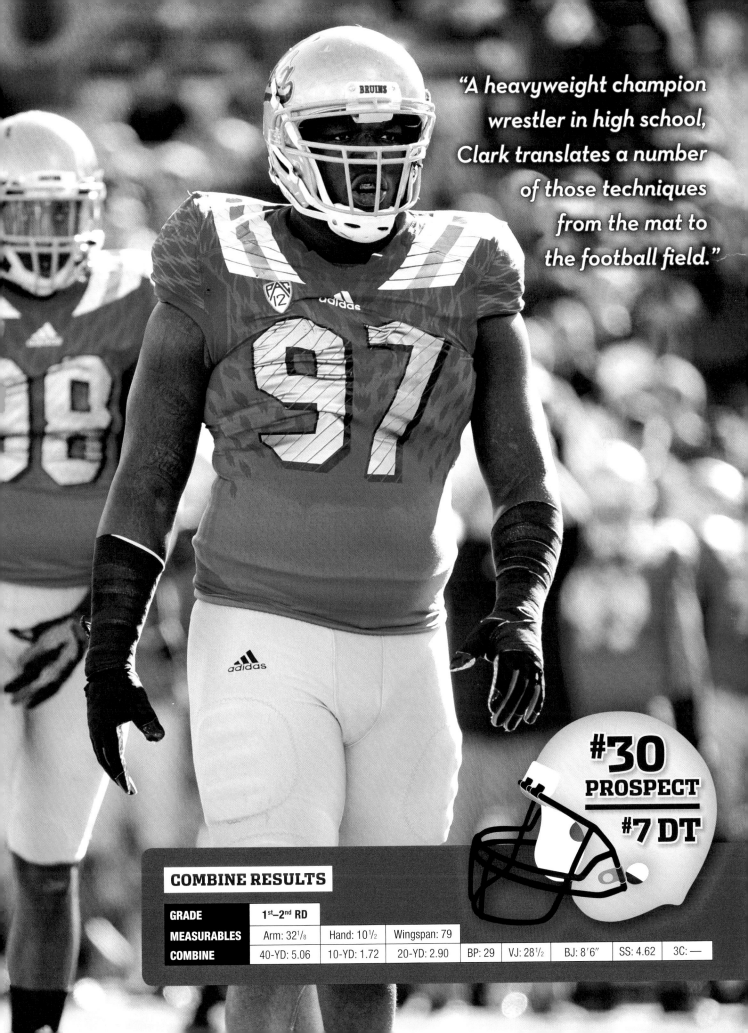

"A heavyweight champion wrestler in high school, Clark translates a number of those techniques from the mat to the football field."

#30 PROSPECT

#7 DT

COMBINE RESULTS

GRADE	1st–2nd RD							
MEASURABLES	Arm: 32⅛	Hand: 10½	Wingspan: 79					
COMBINE	40-YD: 5.06	10-YD: 1.72	20-YD: 2.90	BP: 29	VJ: 28½	BJ: 8'6"	SS: 4.62	3C: —

JACK CONKLIN
OT / MICHIGAN STATE

Name: Jack Conklin

Ht: 6'5¾" **Wt:** 308

Hometown/High School: Plainwell, MI / Plainwell

Class: Redshirt Junior

Number: 74

DOB: August 17, 1994

Career Highlights: All-American (2015), First-Team All–Big Ten (2015), Second-Team All–Big Ten (2014), Freshman All-American (2013)

Did You Know? If selected in the first round, Conklin would be the first Michigan State offensive lineman drafted in the opening round since Tony Mandarich (1989).

Fun Fact: Darren Conklin, Jack's father and high school football coach, was also a walk-on offensive tackle in college, but he was a Wolverine in Ann Arbor.

Ideal Team Fit: A powerfully built college left tackle, Conklin, who is ready for NFL snaps now, plays a physical brand of football better suited for the right side or the interior.

NFL Comparison: Andrew Whitworth

With only one scholarship offer out of high school (Division-II Wayne State), Jack Conklin planned to play the 2012 season at a military academy in an attempt to garner more interest. However, Spartans head coach Mark Dantonio saw more film and invited him to walk on with the promise that he would go on scholarship the following semester. That prudent decision paid off for both Michigan State and Conklin as he blossomed in East Lansing, protecting Connor Cook's blindside. After redshirting in 2012 and earning Freshman All-America honors in 2013, Conklin started all 13 games as a sophomore left tackle and earned second-team All–Big Ten honors. He missed two games due to a knee sprain as a junior, but started 12 games and was named first-team all-conference.

STRENGTHS: Well-built with excellent core strength and center of gravity to stay balanced through contact. Wide base with lower body power to control the point of attack. Strong upper body and hands to jolt and steer defenders as a run blocker. Works hard to keep spacing with his reach. Controlled in space and picks up edge speed, sinking his hips to anchor. Rarely plays in reverse. Smart and instinctive, understanding protections and using his eyes to pick up extra pressures. Aggressive and always looking for someone to block, displaying a dependable playing temperament. Accomplished three-year starter with experience on both sides of the line of scrimmage (38 career starts).

WEAKNESSES: Adequate length, but doesn't play like it, allowing rushers into his body at times in an attempt to control them. Not a light mover and slow to recover once rushers gain a step. Tends to get his feet tied up in his initial kick-slide, lunging and falling off balance. Will open up prematurely and struggle in space. Not a rangy player and too often late to climb to the second level. Technique tends to break down versus speed. Medical reports are important, suffering a left knee sprain (September 2015) that forced him to miss two games.

SUMMARY: A late bloomer who struggled to attract any attention as a high school recruit, Conklin worked his way to a scholarship at Michigan State and is now a legitimate first-round prospect. Conklin is powerful and quick-minded to read/react in a flash and dominate in tight spaces, but he doesn't have the quick-twitch body control to consistently mirror in space. He has some athletic limitations and will struggle with edge speed at times, but no one is going through him due to his wide base and contact balance. Conklin is always in a ready position and rarely seems surprised, which compensates for his lack of elite quickness in pass protection. Powerfully built, well-coached, and a natural competitor, Conklin is thirsty for NFL snaps.

CAREER STATS

SEASON	GP/GS	POS
2012	Redshirted	
2013	14/13	10 LT, 3 RT
2014	13/13	LT
2015	12/12	LT
Career	39/38	35 LT, 3 RT

"Powerfully built, well-coached, and a natural competitor, Conklin is thirsty for NFL snaps."

#31 PROSPECT

#4 OT

COMBINE RESULTS

GRADE	1st–2nd RD							
MEASURABLES	Arm: 35	Hand: 10⅜	Wingspan: 83¼					
COMBINE	40-YD: 5.00	10-YD: 1.76	20-YD: 2.92	BP: 25	VJ: 30	BJ: 8'7"	SS: 4.57	3C: 7.63

MICHAEL THOMAS
WR / OHIO STATE

Name: Michael Thomas

Ht: 6′2¾″ **Wt:** 212

Hometown/High School: Los Angeles, CA / Woodland Hills Taft

Class: Redshirt Junior

Number: 3

DOB: August 16, 1994

Career Highlights: Third-Team All–Big Ten (2015)

Did You Know? The nephew of former No. 1 overall pick and 11-year NFL veteran wide receiver Keyshawn Johnson

Fun Fact: Roomed with future Ohio State teammate and fellow 2016 NFL Draft prospect Cardale Jones at Fork Union Military Academy in 2011.

Ideal Team Fit: Doesn't have the elite speed to stretch the field, but he will be a perfect fit for an offense seeking a complimentary No. 2 possession receiver.

NFL Comparison: A more refined Reuben Randle

A late bloomer out of high school, Michael Thomas wasn't highly recruited and attended Fork Union Military Academy for a year in 2011, attracting much more attention from big-time programs and committing to Ohio State. He saw limited playing time as a true freshman in 2012, then struggled with consistency and academics, leading to the coach's decision to redshirt him in 2013. Thomas returned in 2014 as a sophomore and led the national champion Buckeyes with 54 receptions for 799 yards and nine touchdowns. He produced similar numbers in 2015 with a team-best 56 catches for 781 yards and nine scores, earning third-team All–Big Ten honors.

STRENGTHS: Well-built frame with ideal height and muscle definition for the position. Natural hands to attack the ball away from his body, showing terrific hand-eye coordination. Reliable in 50-50 situations, using his strength and powerful hands to establish body position and out-muscle defensive backs. Strategic route runner and very deliberate in his patterns, using his footwork to get defenders leaning and commit their hips. Determined leaper to high point and an athletic toe-tapper along the sidelines. Uses strong strides to accelerate and pick up speed as he goes. Proved to be a reliable pass-catcher the past two seasons despite limited opportunities due to Ohio State's run-oriented offense.

WEAKNESSES: Lacks above-average start/stop athleticism to easily create outside of the route. Cornerbacks can match his burst and vertical speed, limiting his ability to consistently separate. Not a proven deep threat. Mechanical at times in his movements, lacking ideal lower body fluidity, and not asked to run a diverse route tree in Ohio State's offense. Strong hands, but will have some focus drops, thinking too much about his surroundings. Shows good pop as a blocker, but doesn't consistently sustain. Had trouble picking up the offense early in his career and wasn't asked to be a workhorse receiver (only two career 100-yard receiving games).

SUMMARY: A two-year starter in Ohio State's spread attack, Thomas didn't start full-time in high school until his senior season (caught 21 touchdowns from former Arizona State quarterback Mike Bercovici at Woodland Hills Taft). He spent a year at prep school and two more seasons learning the Buckeyes' offense before emerging as the best Ohio State wide receiver in 2014, leading the team in catches the last two seasons. Thomas isn't the fastest or most explosive wideout, but he is a good-sized athlete and detailed route runner with little wasted movements to create spacing at the stem and stab the ball from the air. Although he will need time to adapt to an NFL playbook, he projects as an ideal No. 2 wide receiver at the next level due to his savvy footwork, body control, and ball skills to be a reliable possession target.

CAREER STATS

SEASON	GP/GS	REC	REC YD	REC AVG	REC TD
2012	11/0	3	22	7.3	0
2013			Redshirted		
2014	15/14	54	799	14.8	9
2015	13/13	56	781	13.9	9
Career	39/27	113	1,602	14.2	18

"Strategic route runner and very deliberate in his patterns, using his footwork to get defenders leaning and commit their hips."

#32
PROSPECT
#3 WR

COMBINE RESULTS

GRADE	1ˢᵗ–2ⁿᵈ RD							
MEASURABLES	Arm: 32¹/₈	Hand: 10¹/₂	Wingspan: 78¹/₄					
COMBINE	40-YD: 4.57	10-YD: 1.55	20-YD: 2.63	BP: 18	VJ: 35	BJ: 10′6″	SS: 4.13	3C: 6.80

PHAROH COOPER
WR / SOUTH CAROLINA

Name: Pharoh Cooper

Ht: 5'11⅛" **Wt:** 203

Hometown/High School: Havelock, NC / Havelock

Class: Junior

Number: 11

DOB: March 7, 1995

Career Highlights: First-Team All-SEC (2015), First-Team All-SEC (2014)

Did You Know? Registered nine 100-yard receiving games the last two seasons, including the South Carolina single-game record of 233 yards against Tennessee in 2014.

Fun Fact: Parents named him "Pharoh" after the Egyptian pharaohs, but his mother thought the second "a" wasn't necessary.

Ideal Team Fit: Similar to the way Green Bay uses Cobb, Cooper can play outside in two-wide receiver sets or inside in the slot when the offense goes to three-receiver looks. His versatility expands his role across multiple NFL schemes.

NFL Comparison: Randall Cobb

Growing up in North Carolina, Pharoh Cooper's dream school was UNC, but because he didn't have a "good feel" with the Tar Heels coaching staff, he spurned their recruitment and signed with South Carolina. He arrived as a safety, but moved to receiver, where he contributed as a true freshman backup. Cooper became a starting wide receiver as a sophomore in 2014 and had a breakout season with 69 catches for 1,136 yards and nine touchdowns (all career highs), earning first-team All-SEC honors. He produced similar numbers as a junior in 2015, leading the Gamecocks with 66 receptions for 973 yards and eight scores to again earn first-team All-SEC honors.

STRENGTHS: Electric athlete with light feet and creative moves, showing the strong strides to accelerate and eliminate pursuit angles. Hits top speed instantly with excellent plant-and-go movements in his routes, not losing any speed in his breaks. Smoothly changes directions without slowing down, allowing him to work back to the ball and separate in his patterns. Terrific vision as a ball carrier and follows blocks well. Quick hands and reliable ball skills to be a catch-and-go threat, showing the focus to pluck poor throws without breaking stride. Plays with a high degree of toughness over the middle and doesn't allow impending contact to spook him. Versatile offensive threat in college with a lot of direct snaps, averaging 7.2 yards per rush and completing 56% of his passes (four touchdown throws). Offers return experience on special teams, averaging 4.7 yards per punt return and 22.4 yards per kickoff return. Humble, high-effort worker and very coachable, growing up in a military family.

WEAKNESSES: Ordinary height and length for the position, limiting his catch radius. Better play speed than timed speed. Wasn't asked to run a sophisticated route tree in college and still learning the nuances at the stem of patterns. Has some double-catches and needs to do a better job tracking over his shoulder. Holds the ball loose and away from his body, leading to ball security concerns (seven career fumbles). Inconsistent on-the-move efficiency as a blocker, showing effort to deliver pop, but struggles to sustain. High volume of touches in college led to physical collisions, limping off the field several times on film.

SUMMARY: A two-year starter, Cooper was a do-everything weapon for the Gamecocks, overcoming poor QB play to earn first-team All-SEC honors as a sophomore and junior. He is a playmaker with the ball in his hands, displaying the play speed, elusive cuts, and start/stop movements to create on his own and generate separation as a route-runner. Despite only average size, Cooper doesn't worry about contact and is always working to get open, never taking a play off. A similar prospect to Randall Cobb out of Kentucky, Cooper is a superb talent and person who will contribute as a jack-of-all-trades for an offense.

CAREER STATS

SEASON	GP/GS	REC	REC YD	REC AVG	REC TD
2013	11/1	3	54	18.0	1
2014	13/12	69	1,136	16.5	9
2015	12/12	66	973	14.7	8
Career	36/25	138	2,163	15.7	18

"He is a playmaker with the ball in his hands, displaying the play speed, elusive cuts, and start/stop movements to create on his own."

#33 PROSPECT

#4 WR

COMBINE RESULTS

GRADE	1ˢᵗ–2ⁿᵈ RD							
MEASURABLES	Arm: 32¼	Hand: 9⅛	Wingspan: 75					
COMBINE	40-YD: —	10-YD: —	20-YD: —	BP: 15	VJ: 31	BJ: 9'7"	SS: —	3C: —

KEVIN DODD
DE / CLEMSON

Name: Kevin Dodd

Ht: 6'5" **Wt:** 277

Hometown/High School: Taylors, SC / Riverside

Class: Redshirt Junior

Number: 98

DOB: July 14, 1992

Career Highlights: Had the best game of his career in the 2016 CFP National Championship Game vs. Alabama, with 3 sacks and 5 tackles for loss

Did You Know? His 23.5 tackles for loss ranked second nationally (behind only Shaq Lawson), but he didn't garner All-ACC honors, mostly because 8.5 of those tackles for loss came in the two College Football Playoff games.

Fun Fact: Standout high school performer in track and field as the Greenville County champion in the shot-put and runner-up in the discus, earning county Field Athlete of the Year.

Ideal Team Fit: Similar to his role at Clemson, he projects best as a left defensive end in a four-man front, fitting teams like the Minnesota Vikings or Miami Dolphins.

NFL Comparison: Kony Ealy

A relative unknown prior to the 2015 season, Kevin Dodd seized his opportunity as a starter opposite Shaq Lawson to form one of the best pass-rush duos in the country. He committed to Clemson out of high school, but didn't qualify academically and spent the 2011 season at Hargrave Military Academy. After enrolling at Clemson in 2012, Dodd was buried on the depth chart and battled injuries early in his career, but with Vic Beasley and Corey Crawford graduating after the 2014 season, he improved his mind-set and training habits to secure Crawford's spot in the starting lineup. Over 15 starts in 2015, Dodd tallied 23.5 tackles for loss and 12 sacks, falling just shy of Lawson's numbers for the team lead.

STRENGTHS: Has the look of an NFL defensive end with broad shoulders and long arms to engage and keep blockers from his body. Flexible body type to plant-and-bend when he wins the corner. Quick first step and lateral inside move to slip blocks, using active hands to fight through jabs. Shows the backfield vision to see through blockers and recognize offensive tendencies with natural instincts. Improved discipline and patience to hold backside contain, stack the edge, and cut off runs to the outside. High motor player and fights through the whistle, wearing down offensive linemen. Pushed himself in the film room and on the practice field to seize his opportunity to start in 2015. Described as a "self-made guy" by Clemson defensive coordinator Brent Venables.

WEAKNESSES: Not a twitched-up rusher who can easily change speeds in his rush, lacking cat-like quickness. Needs to better keep his balance through gaps. Doesn't consistently use his hands to convert speed to power and isn't much of a bully. Undeveloped pass-rush repertoire and needs to add more to his bag of tricks to fool blockers. Tends to over-think and play too patiently at times. Lack of hand tactics will cause his rush to stall. Only one season of starting experience and productivity. Benefited from playing opposite Shaq Lawson, rarely facing double-teams.

SUMMARY: A one-year starter, Dodd lined up in both a two- and three-point stance as the starting left defensive end in Clemson's 4-3 scheme. Based on traits, Dodd checks several boxes for the NFL with the size, length, athleticism, and strength potential to be effective in the NFL. He also improved his ball awareness and discipline as his reps increased last season, showing encouraging growth that indicates he isn't near his football ceiling. An ascending prospect, he isn't a sudden rusher who wins with speed, but he is a promising pass-rush threat due to his snap quickness, natural instincts, and high-effort play style.

CAREER STATS

SEASON	GP/GS	TACKLES	TFL	SACKS	FF
2012	8/0	6	0.0	0.0	0
2013	4/0	7	0.5	*Medical Redshirt*	
2014	12/0	8	2.5	0.0	0
2015	15/15	62	23.5	12.0	1
Career	39/15	83	26.5	12.0	1

"Based on traits, Dodd checks several boxes for the NFL with the size, length, athleticism, and strength potential to be effective in the NFL."

#34
PROSPECT
#6 DE

COMBINE RESULTS

GRADE	1ˢᵗ–2ⁿᵈ RD							
MEASURABLES	Arm: 34	Hand: 10	Wingspan: 81⅝					
COMBINE	40-YD: 4.86	10-YD: 1.69	20-YD: 2.84	BP: —	VJ: —	BJ: —	SS: —	3C: —

VONN BELL
S / OHIO STATE

Name: Vonn Bell

Ht: 5'10¾" **Wt:** 199

Hometown/High School: Rossville, GA / Ridgeland

Class: Junior

Number: 11

DOB: December 12, 1994

Career Highlights: Second-Team All–Big Ten (2015), All-American (2015), CFP National Champion (2015)

Did You Know? His team-leading six interceptions in 2014 for the national champs was the most in a season by an Ohio State player since 2001.

Fun Fact: Vonn's father, Vencent, played linebacker at Murray State for legendary head coach Frank Beamer in the early '80s.

Ideal Team Fit: Bell plays with a decisive reactor and collects himself well in space to line up over the slot as a free safety and nickel cornerback for a team that plays mostly cover-3 looks.

NFL Comparison: Tashaun Gipson

The crown jewel of the Buckeyes' 2013 recruiting class, Vonn Bell held his cards close to his vest, and while most expected the five-star safety to stay in SEC country at Alabama or Tennessee, he went north and enrolled at Ohio State. After a season as a backup, Bell became a full-time starter at safety in 2014 as a sophomore (14 starts) and led the Buckeyes with six interceptions, finishing second on the team with 92 tackles. He started all 13 games as a junior in 2015 and recorded a team-high nine passes defended, adding 65 tackles, and two interceptions to earn second-team All–Big Ten and All-America honors.

STRENGTHS: Good-sized athlete to match up well with receivers. Coordinated athlete with smooth lower-body quickness and hip action to transition with little wasted movement. Drive burst and pursuit speed to close well. Not distracted by eye candy in the backfield, seeing things quickly with the reactive movements to plant, gather, and go. Keeps his weight on the balls of his feet in coverage to stay within arm's reach of the receiver. Reliable ball skills and timing at the catch point and won't cheat his team if he can make a play on the ball. Not a power player, but competes with the toughness to take on blocks and attack as a run defender. Leads with his head/shoulder as a striker and generally gets his man on the ground. Special teams standout and productive as a starter with 22 passes defended and nine interceptions over 28 starts.

WEAKNESSES: Adequate body type and length for the position, but not an intimidating physical presence. Needs to improve his strike zone technique as a run defender, with more ankle-biting tackles than you want to see on film. Inconsistent breaking down in space with a bad habit of waiting on the ball carrier and playing on his heels, causing him to be run over at the contact point. Anticipates well on some snaps, but then late to recognize the play design on others. Can get turned around in coverage and struggles to locate or make plays on the ball once his back is turned to the line of scrimmage. Not a playmaker after the interception, averaging 5.4 yards per return.

SUMMARY: A two-year starter at free safety, Bell lined up mostly as a single-high and nickel safety in Ohio State's secondary and emerged as a defensive playmaker for the Buckeyes during the team's national title run in 2014. (Ohio State head coach Urban Meyer said of Bell, "I've been lucky to have been around a lot of good safeties, and he's as good as I've ever had.") He has room to improve his tackling mechanics, but plays with the requisite mental and physical toughness to be active in run support. Bell is proven on an island, showing athleticism, timing, and savvy that translates well to the next level.

CAREER STATS

SEASON	GP/GS	TACKLES	TFL	SACKS	FF	PASS DEF	INT
2013	14/1	19	1.0	0.0	0	1	1
2014	15/14	92	2.0	1.0	0	12	6
2015	13/13	65	1.0	0.0	0	9	2
Career	42/28	176	4.0	1.0	0	22	9

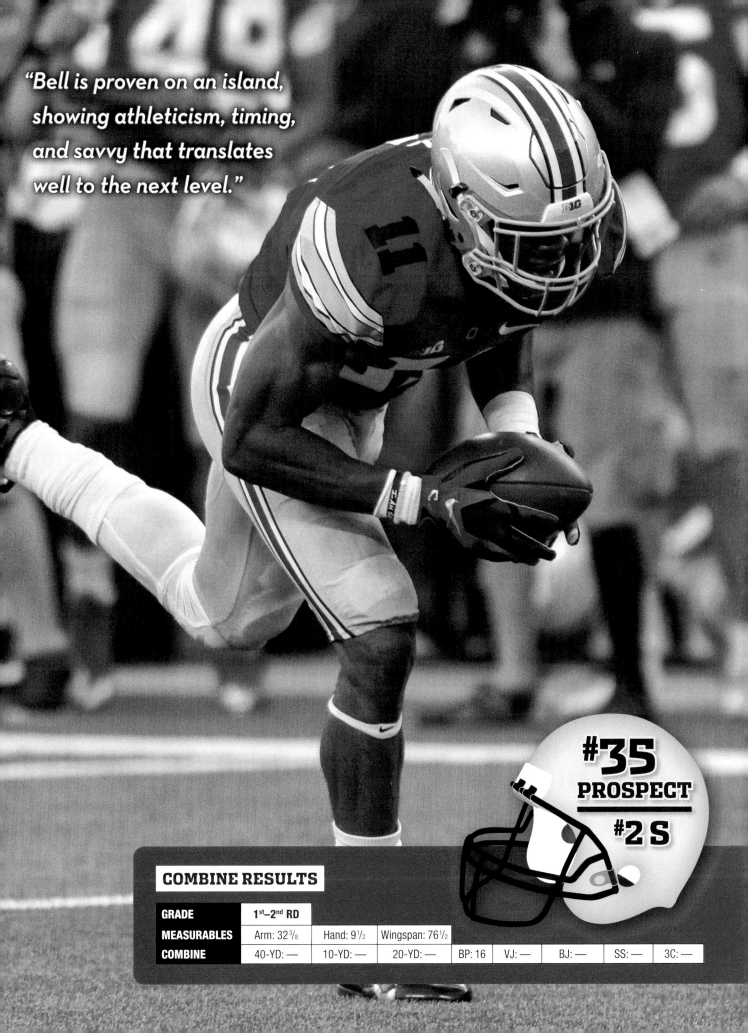

"Bell is proven on an island, showing athleticism, timing, and savvy that translates well to the next level."

#35 PROSPECT

#2 S

COMBINE RESULTS

GRADE	1st–2nd RD							
MEASURABLES	Arm: 32⅜	Hand: 9½	Wingspan: 76½					
COMBINE	40-YD: —	10-YD: —	20-YD: —	BP: 16	VJ: —	BJ: —	SS: —	3C: —

SU'A CRAVENS
LB / USC

Name: Su'a Cravens

Ht: 6'3/4" **Wt:** 226

Hometown/High School: Los Angeles, CA / Vista Murrieta

Class: Junior

Number: 21

DOB: July 7, 1995

Career Highlights: First-Team All-Pac-12 (2015), All-American (2015), First-Team All-Pac-12 (2014), All-American (2014), All-Pac-12 Honorable Mention (2013), Freshman All-American (2013)

Did You Know? Cravens announced his college commitment on his mother's birthday (June 6, 2012) and his declaration for the 2016 NFL Draft on his father's birthday (December 16, 2015).

Fun Fact: His brother (football) and sister (basketball) both played at Hawaii and he has multiple cousins who played football collegiately and now in the NFL, including tight end Jordan Cameron and linebacker Manti Te'o.

Ideal Team Fit: His positional fit in the NFL will vary by scheme with some pro scouts viewing him as a strong safety and others as a weak-side linebacker, but creative coordinators will figure out how to maximize his savvy instincts and athleticism in any defense.

NFL Comparison: Shaq Thompson

The Trojans' best player the past few seasons, Su'a Cravens was a five-star recruit and the top prep player in the state of California, living up to the extraordinary hype at USC. He started at strong safety as a true freshman and recorded 52 tackles and four interceptions, earning numerous Freshman All-America honors. Cravens moved to a hybrid linebacker/safety role in 2014 as a sophomore and showed off his versatility by leading the team in tackles for loss (17) and interceptions (3). He started all 14 games as a junior and led the Trojans in tackles (86), tackles for loss (15), sacks (5.5), and forced fumbles (2), earning first-team All-Pac-12 and All-America honors for the second straight year.

STRENGTHS: Fluid athlete for his size who flawlessly transfers his weight in his movements. Explosive burst to beat blockers to the spot with controlled pursuit speed. Diagnoses quickly with an attacking mind-set and reactive athleticism. High football IQ, anticipation, and sense of his surroundings. Comfortable in space and can cover a lot of green, staying in phase with receivers in man coverage or making stops versus the run. Great job leveraging blocks and will sacrifice himself to give his teammates a chance to make the play. Savvy blitzer and takes correct pursuit angles. Versatile skill-set and played all over the USC defense as a safety, linebacker, and cornerback—also played on special teams coverages. Team captain who eats, drinks, and breathes football.

WEAKNESSES: Lean-muscled and lacks an ideal build for linebacker. Core strength doesn't always match his intentions. Improved fundamental tackler, but still undisciplined in areas and has some bad habits that will lead to missed tackles—tends to drop his head and isn't a wrap, lift, and drive player. Can be engulfed and eaten up near the line of scrimmage, struggling to take on bigger bodies. Aggressive nature will lead to negative plays. Played most of his USC career near the line of scrimmage and was rarely in the deep half of the field. Positional fit is a question mark for some schemes. Missed only one game the past three seasons, but parts of several other games due to injuries, lacking ideal body armor for the position.

SUMMARY: A three-year starter, Cravens began his career at strong safety before moving to a hybrid strong-side linebacker position in the Trojans' 3-4 base defense, where he was asked to do a little bit of everything, playing mostly at the line. His take-on strength and tackling are both average for the position, but he's a fluid athlete with excellent reaction skills who can cover wide receivers on an island. His best traits are his instincts to anticipate the play and always be around the ball—whether at linebacker or safety, Cravens is consistently in the right place at the right time, and that's not an accident.

CAREER STATS

SEASON	GP/GS	TACKLES	TFL	SACKS	FF	INT
2013	13/13	52	1.5	0.0	1	4
2014	13/13	68	17.0	5.0	0	3
2015	14/14	86	15.0	5.5	2	2
Career	40/40	206	33.5	10.5	3	9

"Whether at linebacker or safety, Cravens is consistently in the right place at the right time, and that's not an accident."

#36 PROSPECT

#5 LB

COMBINE RESULTS

GRADE	1st–2nd RD							
MEASURABLES	Arm: 32⅛	Hand: 9½	Wingspan: 78					
COMBINE	40-YD: —	10-YD: —	20-YD: —	BP: 16	VJ: 27	BJ: 9'6"	SS: —	3C: —

AUSTIN JOHNSON
DT / PENN STATE

Name: Austin Johnson

Ht: 6'4⅜" **Wt:** 314

Hometown/High School: Galloway, NJ / St. Augustine Prep

Class: Redshirt Junior

Number: 99

DOB: May 8, 1994

Career Highlights: Senior Bowl (2016), Third-Team All–Big Ten (2015)

Did You Know? Graduated with a degree in broadcast journalism and hopes to be a sports announcer after his playing career is complete.

Fun Fact: His first love is basketball, and his younger sister, Kennedy, is a sophomore on the Michigan State women's team.

Ideal Team Fit: Due to his natural power and athleticism, Johnson will be appealing to both 3-4 and 4-3 schemes, either over the center or the A-gap.

NFL Comparison: Eddie Goldman

A Penn State fan growing up, Austin Johnson was under-recruited out of high school, so he was thrilled to receive scholarship offers from schools like Boston College and Rutgers. But the day the Nittany Lions offered him, Johnson accepted. He started a pair of games in 2013 as a redshirt freshman, recording 27 tackles, three tackles for loss, and a sack. Johnson became a full-time starter in 2014 as a sophomore and collected 49 tackles, six tackles for loss, and one sack. He had his best season as a junior in 2015 (13 starts), finishing third on the team with 78 tackles, 15 tackles for loss, and 6.5 sacks to earn third-team All–Big Ten honors.

STRENGTHS: Thick body type with broad shoulders and meaty lower body. Core strength and flexibility to stack and anchor double-teams. Moves well for his size with natural body control and smooth hip action. Carries his weight well to mirror up and down the line of scrimmage, offering pass rush value due to his lateral agility to sidestep blockers. Balanced feet in space and through congestion. Heavy-handed to generate push and work his way through bodies. Active with his limbs to snatch and stash, playing with violence to press blockers from his frame. Improved ball awareness to quickly locate and hustle in pursuit. Highly productive in 2015, finishing third on the team in tackles (78), and was one of only three interior defensive linemen at the FBS level who tallied at least 15 tackles for loss in 2015. Durable and started every game the last two seasons, rarely leaving the field.

WEAKNESSES: Only average initial quickness and snap anticipation. Inconsistent pad level and plays too high, struggling to routinely sink. Overaggressive in pursuit and needs to play more controlled in small spaces. Requires mechanical development, especially with his hand placement and reach to keep separation from blockers. Effort isn't a question as a pass rusher, but needs to better mix up his moves and put more thought into his sequence, including an effective counter move. Not a rangy player and has a small radius of impact. Productive tackler and strong finisher, but needs to better reset and break down in motion.

SUMMARY: A two-year starter at Penn State, Johnson lined up mostly as a nose and one-technique tackle. While defensive linemates Carl Nassib and Anthony Zettel would often rotate in and out, Johnson rarely left the field. He has well-distributed mass and holds up well versus multiple blockers to clog the middle of the field and mirror ball carriers. Although not a rangy player, his motor is always revving, and he moves well in small areas with strong hands to stack and create movement. A player whose production matches the tape, Johnson has an impressive blend of power, quickness, and awareness to fit even and odd fronts.

CAREER STATS

SEASON	GP/GS	TACKLES	TFL	SACKS	FF
2012	Redshirted				
2013	12/2	27	3.0	1.0	0
2014	13/13	49	6.0	1.0	0
2015	13/13	78	15.0	6.5	1
Career	38/28	154	24.0	8.5	1

"A player whose production matches the tape, Johnson has an impressive blend of power, quickness, and awareness to fit both even and odd fronts."

#37 PROSPECT

#8 DT

COMBINE RESULTS

GRADE	1st–2nd RD							
MEASURABLES	Arm: 32¾	Hand: 9⅞	Wingspan: 77⅜					
COMBINE	40-YD: 5.32	10-YD: 1.85	20-YD: 3.07	BP: 25	VJ: 26	BJ: 8'3"	SS: 4.75	3C: 7.84

RYAN KELLY
C / ALABAMA

Name: Ryan Kelly

Ht: 6'4" **Wt:** 311

Hometown/High School: West Chester, OH / Lakota West

Class: Redshirt Senior

Number: 70

DOB: May 30, 1993

Career Highlights: CFP National Champion (2016), Rimington Trophy (2015), Jacobs Blocking Trophy (2015), Consensus All-American (2015), First-Team All-SEC (2015), SEC Scholar Athlete of the Year (2015)

Did You Know? Cleaned up on the awards circuit in 2015, but being voted an Alabama senior captain by his teammates was his "most valued honor."

Fun Fact: Bypassed his December 2015 master's graduation to attend his first Army-Navy game and watch his younger brother, a junior linebacker for the Midshipmen.

Ideal Team Fit: A scheme-versatile pivot, Kelly might never be an All-Pro, but he will play in the NFL for the next decade, fitting any offense with an immediate need for a starting center.

NFL Comparison: Corey Linsley

The glue of the Alabama offensive line in 2015, Ryan Kelly didn't allow a sack as a senior and paved the way for running back Derrick Henry to set a new SEC rushing record and win the Heisman Trophy. He took over the starting duties in 2013 and started 21 games combined as a sophomore and junior. Kelly started all 15 games for the national champion Crimson Tide in 2015, earning consensus All-America honors. He also won the Rimington Trophy as the Nation's top center and the Jacobs Blocking Trophy as the top offensive lineman in the conference.

STRENGTHS: Quick snap-and-step, sitting in his stance to anchor, absorb contact, and push back. Proper bend below the waist to maintain leverage and get underneath defenders. Extends well to keep defenders from his frame and works hard to gain body position. Patience in space to attack the second level. Moves well laterally to pull and work around bodies. Noticeably stronger as a senior. Naturally instinctive to anticipate pre-snap and on the move. Highly intelligent, both on and off the field—named the 2015 SEC Scholar-Athlete of the Year. Made all the calls on the Alabama offensive line, getting everyone lined up and communicating well. Very detailed with a tough demeanor, battling through the whistle. Accountable, no-nonsense leader and voted a team captain in 2015. Seasoned veteran with 36 starts under his belt in the SEC.

WEAKNESSES: Average-at-best size, length, and growth potential—needs to continue and develop his power. Quick movements based more on awareness rather than explosive traits. Overeager at times and needs to stay off the ground, lunging, dropping his eyes and falling off his target. Overaggressive at the second level, leading to his pads rising or overrunning linebackers. Needs to improve his timing in space to land blocks on designed screens. Durability hasn't been a strength, missing four games in September 2013 (stretched MCL), two games in October 2014 (right knee sprain) and most of the Texas A&M contest this past season due to a concussion (October 2015).

SUMMARY: A three-year starter, Kelly took over the pivot duties at Alabama after Barrett Jones graduated and developed into one of the best centers in the country—described as the "heart and soul" of the offense by Heisman-winning running back Derrick Henry. He plays with more hustle than physical talent, but has a strong understanding of how to use his positional skill and smarts to complete the mission. Although he rarely moves bodies in the run game, Kelly engages well on combo blocks and gains position, using his awareness to be a model of consistency. He is the ultimate lunch-pail worker with the competitive grit and IQ that translates well to the pro game.

CAREER STATS

SEASON	GP/GS	POS
2012	10/0	C
2013	9/9	C
2014	12/12	C
2015	15/15	C
Career	46/36	C

"He is the ultimate lunch-pail worker with the competitive grit and IQ that translates well to the pro game."

#38 PROSPECT

#1 C

COMBINE RESULTS

GRADE	1st–2nd RD							
MEASURABLES	Arm: 33⅝	Hand: 9⅝	Wingspan: 80⅝					
COMBINE	40-YD: 5.03	10-YD: 1.76	20-YD: 2.93	BP: 26	VJ: 30	BJ: 8'7"	SS: 4.59	3C: 7.58

KAMALEI CORREA
DE / BOISE STATE

Name: Kamalei Correa

Ht: 6'2⅝" **Wt:** 243

Hometown/High School: Honolulu, HI / Saint Louis School

Class: Junior

Number: 8

DOB: April 27, 1994

Career Highlights: Second-Team All–Mountain West (2015), First-Team All–Mountain West (2014)

Did You Know? Boise State has now lost an underclassman to the NFL Draft each of the last three years (2015: Jay Ajayi, Miami Dolphins; 2014: Demarcus Lawrence, Dallas Cowboys).

Fun Fact: Correa received a scholarship offer at the age of 15 from Hawaii where his two older brothers played on the defensive line and his mother worked for the athletic department.

Ideal Team Fit: With his tweener size, Correa is at his best in space and ideally suited for a 3-4 scheme where he can generate pressure, but his versatility should grow as he develops in the NFL.

NFL Comparison: Rob Ninkovich

A three-star defensive end recruit out of high school, Kamalei Correa (KAH-muh-lay / corr-AY-uh) committed to Boise State over several Pac-12 programs like Arizona, Arizona State, and Utah. He served as a true freshman backup in 2013 and recorded 12 tackles, 1.5 tackles for loss, and one sack. Correa became a starter in 2014 as a sophomore (14 starts) and led the team in tackles for loss (19) and sacks (12), earning first-team All–Mountain West honors. He again started every game as a junior in 2015 (13 starts) and led the team in tackles for loss (11), sacks (7), and forced fumbles (3), earning second-team All–Mountain West honors.

STRENGTHS: Quick-footed athlete with the fluid lower body to move laterally around blocks and scream through gaps. Above average short-area burst and balance, changing his speeds well in his movements to keep blockers guessing. Impressive initial get-off to attack upfield in a blink, working his inside shoulder past the outside shoulder of the blocker. Fast eyes to make snap decisions on the fly, breaking down well in space. Shows the ability to extend, snatch, and toss with aggressive hands to jolt at the point of attack. Moves well in reverse to drop and cover zones in the middle of the field. Physical striker with lift-and-drive technique to be a finisher once he makes contact. High-effort hustler with the competitive fire that sustains all four quarters. Productive the past two seasons as a starter, leading the team in sacks and tackles for loss both years.

WEAKNESSES: Tweener size, length, and growth potential. Lacks the hand strength to rip through or overwhelm blockers. Struggles to consistently stack and detach himself from blocks on the edge. Relies on his lower body to penetrate the pocket, not his upper body mechanics or power. Needs to develop his take-on technique. Can be moved at the point of attack in the run game, especially by double-teams. Unpolished pass-rush moves and sequence. Needs to recognize play designs and screens quicker.

SUMMARY: A two-year starter, Correa lined up as the "stud" defensive end in Boise State's versatile 3-4 scheme, playing with his hand on the ground and standing off the line of scrimmage. He is a loose-hipped athlete with the sudden quickness and lateral agility to work his way around bodies and threaten the pocket. Correa is aggressive at the point of attack, but he can be washed out of the hole due to his average strength and stack-shed technique for the trenches. His pass-rush arsenal lacks variety at this point in his development, and his production is based more on effort and raw athleticism than technique and discipline. However, Correa is only scratching the surface of his ability and shows the athleticism and competitive toughness to be a productive NFL pass rusher.

CAREER STATS

SEASON	GP/GS	TACKLES	TFL	SACKS	FF
2013	13/0	12	1.5	1.0	0
2014	14/14	59	19.0	12.0	2
2015	13/13	39	11.0	7.0	3
Career	40/27	110	31.5	20.0	5

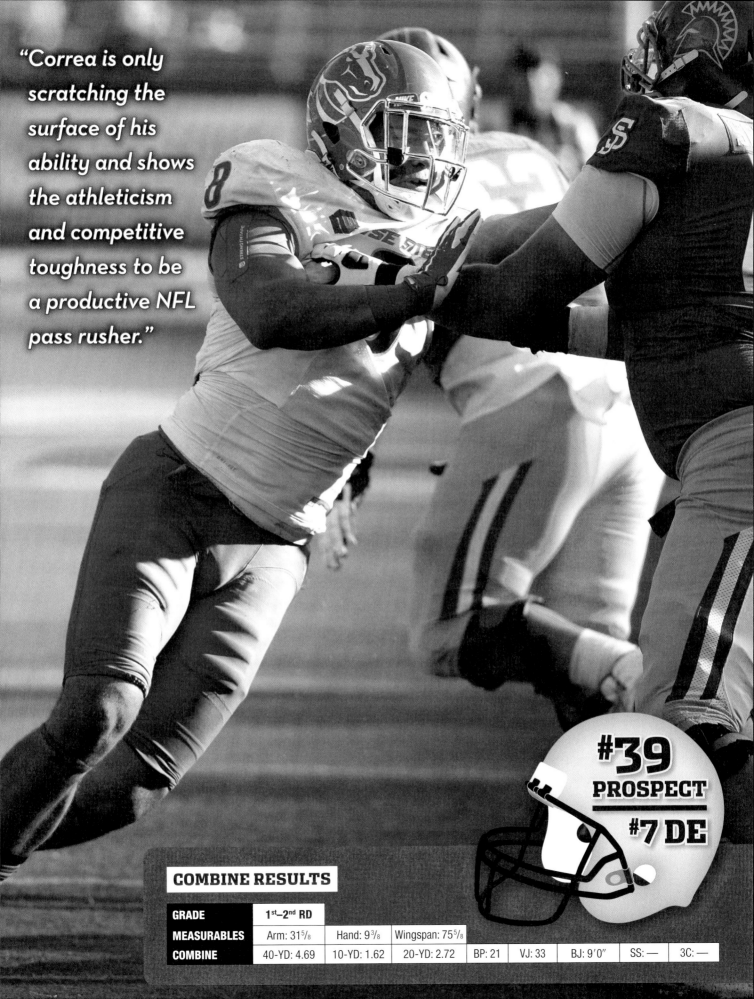

"Correa is only scratching the surface of his ability and shows the athleticism and competitive toughness to be a productive NFL pass rusher."

#39 PROSPECT

#7 DE

COMBINE RESULTS

GRADE	1st–2nd RD							
MEASURABLES	Arm: 31⅝	Hand: 9⅜	Wingspan: 75⅝					
COMBINE	40-YD: 4.69	10-YD: 1.62	20-YD: 2.72	BP: 21	VJ: 33	BJ: 9'0"	SS: —	3C: —

KENDALL FULLER
CB / VIRGINIA TECH

Name: Kendall Fuller

Ht: 5′11½″ **Wt:** 187

Hometown/High School: Baltimore, MD / Our Lady of Good Counsel

Class: Junior

Number: 11

DOB: February 13, 1995

Career Highlights: First-Team All-ACC (2014), All-American (2014), All-American (2013), ACC Freshman of the Year (2013)

Did You Know? Once drafted, Kendall will be the fourth Fuller brother selected in the NFL Draft, joining Kyle (2014, first round, Chicago Bears), Corey (2013, sixth round, Detroit Lions), and Vincent (2005, fourth round, Tennessee Titans).

Fun Fact: If selected in the top 31 picks, Kendall and Kyle Fuller would join Chris and Kyle Long as the only set of brothers currently in the NFL who were both drafted in round one.

Ideal Team Fit: With his size, skill-set, and tackling ability, Fuller best fits off-man and zone coverages and is the type of prospect teams like the Pittsburgh Steelers, who run a lot of cover-2 looks, will be interested in.

NFL Comparison: Tramon Williams

With the last name of Fuller, was there any doubt where Kendall was going to play his college football? A five-star cornerback recruit, he had his choice of schools, but committed to Virginia Tech, where his three older brothers starred before him. Fuller made an instant impact as a true freshman, leading the team with 17 passes defended and six interceptions to earn conference Freshman of the Year honors. He started every game as a sophomore and again led the Hokies in passes defended, adding a pair of interceptions to take home All-America honors. Fuller suffered a knee injury over the summer, but started the first three games of the 2015 season before electing to have season-ending surgery.

STRENGTHS: Solidly built for the position with adequate height and length. Agile, coordinated footwork to mirror, staying low in his pedal and collecting his feet. Smooth athleticism and hip action, using his body position well to leverage and pinch receivers against the sideline. Above-average read/react skills to diagnose off the ball, showing a patient but decisive plant, gather, and go process. Stings in run support and plays with a physical attitude. Natural ball skills and aggressiveness, doing receiver-like things at the catch point. Alert and always looking for work. Coachable and studious, working to hone his craft. His intelligence and intangibles are his best traits, according to the Hokies' coaching staff.

WEAKNESSES: Good enough speed for the position, but NFL receivers will be able to gain a step on him vertically. More smooth than twitchy, giving up separation at times to proficient route runners. Prefers to play the receiver and doesn't consistently get his head turned to find the football in time. Needs to stay balanced with his jam at the line of scrimmage. Handsy downfield and still learning what he can get away with to avoid penalties. Needs to better protect his body to stay unglued from blocks. Medical reports are important after suffering a torn meniscus in his right knee (August 2015), which required season-ending surgery.

SUMMARY: A three-year starter, Fuller has three older brothers who starred at Virginia Tech and were drafted into the NFL, but Kendall was tabbed early on as the most talented football player in the Fuller family, and his film shows why. He looked like a future high-round pick his first two years in Blacksburg, but 2015 was a lost season for him due to a torn meniscus, making his medical reports an essential part of his evaluation. Although his game still needs refinement in areas, Fuller has very good short-area quickness with the controlled footwork, natural feel in coverage, and steadfast self-confidence to develop into a reliable NFL starter.

CAREER STATS

SEASON	GP/GS	TACKLES	TFL	SACKS	FF	PASS DEF	INT
2013	13/12	58	2.5	0.5	1	17	6
2014	13/13	54	4.5	2.0	0	17	2
2015	3/3	7	1.0	1.0	1	1	0
Career	29/28	119	8.0	3.5	2	35	8

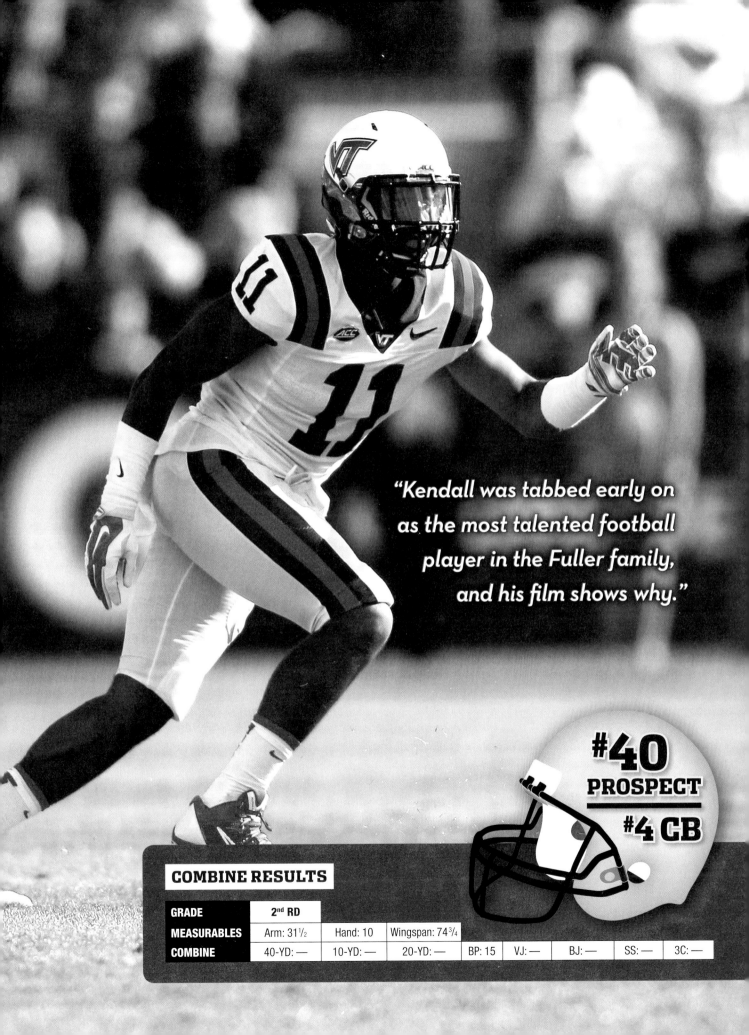

"Kendall was tabbed early on as the most talented football player in the Fuller family, and his film shows why."

#40 PROSPECT
#4 CB

COMBINE RESULTS

GRADE	2ⁿᵈ RD							
MEASURABLES	Arm: 31½	Hand: 10	Wingspan: 74¾					
COMBINE	40-YD: —	10-YD: —	20-YD: —	BP: 15	VJ: —	BJ: —	SS: —	3C: —

EMMANUEL OGBAH
DE / OKLAHOMA STATE

Name: Emmanuel Ogbah

Ht: 6′4¼″ **Wt:** 273

Hometown/High School: Houston, TX / George Bush

Class: Redshirt Junior

Number: 38

DOB: November 6, 1993

Career Highlights: First-Team All–Big 12 (2015), Big 12 Defensive Player of the Year (2015), First-Team All–Big 12 (2014), Big 12 Defensive Lineman of the Year (2014)

Did You Know? Attended the same high school as former Oklahoma State All-American Russell Okung, who is also of Nigerian descent.

Fun Fact: His parents gave him the middle name Ikechukwu (ee-KEH-choo-quoo), which means "God's power" in Igbo, a Nigerian language.

Ideal Team Fit: Can stand up and play in space, but Ogbah is best in a four-man front with his hand on the ground, fitting a team like the Carolina Panthers or New York Giants.

NFL Comparison: Vinny Curry

Born and raised in Lagos, Nigeria, Emmanuel Ogbah moved to Houston at the age of nine in 2004 along with his family for the opportunity of a better life. Although late to the game of football, he proved to be a quick study and earned a scholarship to Oklahoma State, redshirting in 2012. Ogbah became a starter in 2014 as a sophomore and was named Big 12 Defensive Lineman of the Year with 17 tackles for loss and 11 sacks, earning first-team All–Big 12 and Defensive Team MVP honors. He returned in 2015 as a junior and became the first Oklahoma State player to earn Big 12 Defensive Player of the Year honors, recording 64 tackles, 17.5 tackles for loss, 13 sacks, and three forced fumbles.

STRENGTHS: Built well for the position with proportionate bulk and long arms. Easy release out of his stance with natural body control and flexibility to dip around the corner without slowing his momentum. Low, powerful lean into blockers with an improved sense of leverage. Balanced to keep his feet with loose joints to smoothly change directions. Easy lateral quickness to cross the face of blockers, drop in space, or move up and down the line of scrimmage. Strong hands to generate push and rip through blocks, not allowing blockers to dictate his path. Physical tackler who uses his entire body to finish. Disciplined and trusts his coaching. Not the loudest player on the team, but a strong lead-by-example type. Never shuts it down, with outstanding hustle to chase down plays from behind. Reliable personal character, not a player you have to worry about away from the facility.

WEAKNESSES: Only average speed and explosive traits for the position. Still learning how to string together pass-rush moves and connect the dots. Flashes violence in his hands, but needs to better lock out to control the point of attack and move blockers from their spot. Can be slowed at contact and needs to improve his shed technique to keep his rush from stalling. Hand tactics and creativity off the ball lack polish. Needs to better break down when on the move, overrunning the pocket or sliding off ball carriers.

SUMMARY: A two-year starter, Ogbah lined up at both right and left defensive end in Oklahoma State's 4-3 base scheme, primarily in a three-point stance and occasionally standing off the edge. He leaves Stillwater with 28 sacks and 40 tackles for loss, ranking top five in school history in both categories. He is a "coach's dream," according to Cowboys head coach Mike Gundy due to the strong work ethic, acumen, and discipline that were instilled in him at a young age. He is still learning the complexities of the position and lacks elite explosiveness, but Ogbah is a balanced athlete for his size with the physicality and coachable mentality that can be molded in the NFL.

CAREER STATS

SEASON	GP/GS	TACKLES	TFL	SACKS	FF
2012	Redshirted				
2013	13/0	20	5.5	4.0	0
2014	13/13	49	17.0	11.0	1
2015	13/13	64	17.5	13.0	3
Career	39/26	133	40.0	28.0	4

"Ogbah is a balanced athlete for his size with the physicality and coachable mentality that can be molded in the NFL."

#41 PROSPECT

#8 DE

COMBINE RESULTS

GRADE	2nd							
MEASURABLES	Arm: 35½	Hand: 10	Wingspan: 83⅞					
COMBINE	40-YD: 4.63	10-YD: 1.58	20-YD: 2.68	BP: 20	VJ: 35½	BJ: 10'1"	SS: 4.50	3C: 7.26

RASHARD HIGGINS
WR / COLORADO STATE

Name: Rashard Higgins

Ht: 6'1⅜" **Wt:** 196

Hometown/High School: Dallas, TX / Mesquite

Class: Junior

Number: 82

DOB: October 7, 1994

Career Highlights: First-Team All–Mountain West (2015), Consensus All-American (2014), Biletnikoff Award Finalist (2014), First-Team All–Mountain West (2014)

Did You Know? Higgins was a finalist for the Biletnikoff Award (nation's top receiver) in 2014 along with Alabama's Amari Cooper and West Virginia's Kevin White, who were both drafted in the top 10 of the 2015 NFL Draft.

Fun Fact: While humble in nature, Higgins doesn't shy away from his "Hollywood" nickname, which he earned as a child due to his athleticism and charismatic smile.

Ideal Team Fit: Higgins will likely never be a prototypical No. 1 in the NFL, but he can settle into a secondary role due to his ability to exploit holes in the defense and move the chains.

NFL Comparison: Allen Hurns

The most productive wideout in school history, Rashard Higgins was barely a blip on the recruiting radar out of high school and was ready to enroll at FCS-level Sam Houston State until Colorado State swooped in before signing day. He made an instant impact as a true freshman, leading the team with 837 receiving yards on 68 catches. But he had his best season as a sophomore in 2014 with an NCAA-best 1,750 receiving yards and 17 touchdowns—both single-season CSU records. He lost his QB to the NFL (Garrett Grayson, third-round pick of the New Orleans Saints), but Higgins again led the team in receiving as a junior, with 66 catches for 933 yards and eight TDs.

STRENGTHS: Good height and length for the position. Nimble with easy strides and natural body control. Excellent rhythm and depth in his routes, transitioning his weight well. Crafty, coordinated footwork at the top of routes and off the line of scrimmage to create spacing. Above-average locating ability with terrific sight adjustments to find, track, and quickly adjust to the ball. Great sense of surroundings with an innate feel for holes in coverage. Nifty and creative to be a catch-and-go threat. Attacks with his hands and finishes through the process of the catch. Competitive blocker, using his body as a tool. Fearless over the middle and not intimidated by anyone on the field. Carries himself with a quiet confidence and wants to be great. Highly productive and leaves Colorado State as the school's all-time leader in catches (230), receiving yards (3,520), 100-yard receiving games (18), and touchdowns (31).

WEAKNESSES: Thin-boned with lean muscle tone. Not a powerful runner and won't consistently break tackles. Focused, but too finesse at the catch point. Can be overmatched physically and rerouted by some DBs. Mediocre top-end speed and lacks multiple gears. Good plant-and-go quickness, but not naturally explosive or a strong leaper. Has cut down the drops, but will have occasional focus lapses. Doesn't have any return experience on special teams.

SUMMARY: A three-year starter, Higgins made an instant impact at Colorado State, leading the team in receiving each of his three seasons in Fort Collins. He lined up primarily as the "X" receiver in Colorado State's offense and was asked to run a variety of routes, showing the instincts to exploit holes and get uncovered. Higgins isn't a burner or sudden athlete, but he plays with synchronized shake and terrific footwork to plant and go without wasted movements in his routes. He is advanced in several areas at the position and might be the best receiver in this class at improvising to find open zones and give his quarterback a clean target. Although his lack of ideal size and speed will ding him on draft boards, Higgins has the production that matches the tape, and his strengths translate well to the next level.

CAREER STATS

SEASON	GP/GS	REC	REC YD	REC AVG	REC TD
2013	14/14	68	837	12.3	6
2014	12/12	96	1,750	18.2	17
2015	12/11	66	933	14.1	8
Career	38/37	230	3,520	15.3	31

"He is advanced in several areas at the position and might be the best receiver in this class at improvising to find open zones and give his quarterback a clean target."

#42 PROSPECT

#5 WR

COMBINE RESULTS

GRADE	2nd							
MEASURABLES	Arm: 32¼	Hand: 9¾	Wingspan: 76½					
COMBINE	40-YD: 4.64	10-YD: 1.63	20-YD: 2.70	BP: 13	VJ: 32	BJ: 9'8"	SS: —	3C: —

HUNTER HENRY
TE / ARKANSAS

Name: Hunter Henry

Ht: 6′4⅞″ **Wt:** 250

Hometown/High School: Little Rock, AR / Pulaski Academy

Class: Junior

Number: 84

DOB: December 7, 1994

Career Highlights: John Mackey Award (2015), First-Team All-SEC (2015), Second-Team All-SEC (2014), Freshman All-SEC (2013)

Did You Know? Strong understanding of where the sticks are and was a reliable third-down target with 93 of his 116 career catches resulting in a first down or touchdown.

Fun Fact: His father (Mark) was a two-time All-Southwest offensive lineman at Arkansas (1988–1991), but chose to enter the ministry instead of the NFL.

Ideal Team Fit: For a team looking for a plug-and-play inline blocker, Henry isn't for them. But for a team that needs a reliable joker tight end who can impact the passing game, Henry is the top option in the 2016 class.

NFL Comparison: Owen Daniels

After growing up in Atlanta, Hunter Henry moved to Little Rock prior to his freshman year in high school, starring as a tight end first at Pulaski Academy and then for the Razorbacks. He saw immediate playing time as a true freshman (seven starts) in 2013, recording 28 catches for 409 yards and four touchdowns, earning All-SEC Freshman honors. Henry started 10 games as a sophomore in 2014 and finished with 37 receptions for 513 yards and two scores, earning second-team All-SEC honors. He had his best production as a junior in 2015 (13 starts) with 51 catches for 739 yards and three touchdowns, earning first-team All-SEC honors and winning the 2015 John Mackey Award as the Nation's top tight end.

STRENGTHS: Adequate height and length for the position. Terrific athlete for his size with enough speed to separate in his routes. Fluid pass-catcher with flexible body control to easily adjust to throws. Immediately turns downfield and is dangerous after the catch due to his toughness and agility. Shows measured footwork in his breaks and looks comfortable facing every type of defender. Natural hands-catcher, tracking well in his pattern and high-pointing in contested situations. Tough finisher and rarely drops the ball. High-effort blocker with the hustle to get downfield, working through the whistle with the same competitive demeanor. Experienced lining up inline and in the slot and has been lauded by his coaches for his team-oriented mind-set.

WEAKNESSES: Lacks ideal bulk and muscle tone for the position and is still growing into his body. Struggles to establish body position as a blocker and ends up going where the defender wants due to his lack of core strength. Too easily overmatched at the point of attack, struggling to sustain or control blocks. Tends to get grabby and wild in pass protection and has too many snaps on film that will be penalized in the NFL. Only nine career touchdowns in 30 starts and wasn't used as consistent red zone threat.

SUMMARY: A three-year starter, Henry was an ideal fit for the Razorbacks' multiple–tight end offense with pro-style looks that asked him to line up inline, wing, and in the slot. He has the acceleration and body control to be a mismatch against linebackers and the natural strength to overpower defensive backs before and after the catch. Henry has vacuum hands (didn't have a drop in 2015) with fluid body adjustments to catch the ball in stride and track the ball into his mitts. He is a competitive blocker, but too easily overpowered at the point of attack, leading to his getting beat or penalized. Although he's not a reliable inline blocker at this point in his development, Henry knows how to get open and has the best hands and route-running athleticism at tight end in this draft class.

CAREER STATS

SEASON	GP/GS	REC	REC YD	REC AVG	REC TD
2013	12/7	28	409	14.6	4
2014	13/10	37	513	13.9	2
2015	13/13	51	739	14.5	3
Career	38/30	116	1,661	14.3	9

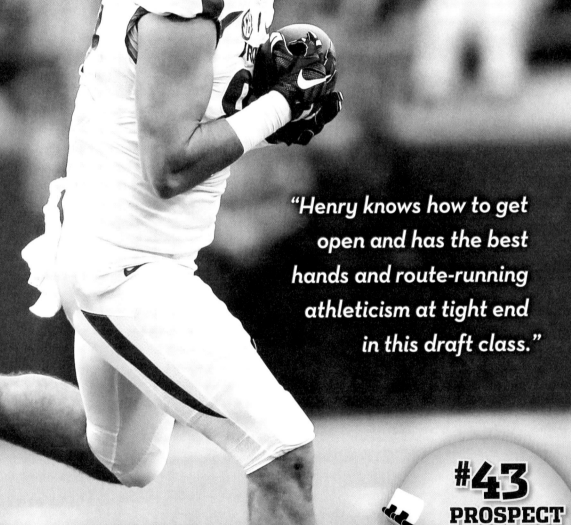

"Henry knows how to get open and has the best hands and route-running athleticism at tight end in this draft class."

#43 PROSPECT
#1 TE

COMBINE RESULTS

GRADE	2nd							
MEASURABLES	Arm: 32¾	Hand: 9¼	Wingspan: 78					
COMBINE	40-YD: —	10-YD: —	20-YD: —	BP: 13	VJ: —	BJ: —	SS: —	3C: —

WILL FULLER
WR / NOTRE DAME

Name: Will Fuller

Ht: 6'1⅛" **Wt:** 186

Hometown/High School: Philadelphia, PA / Roman Catholic

Class: Redshirt Junior

Number: 7

DOB: April 16, 1994

Career Highlights: All-American (2015), All-American (2014)

Did You Know? Leaves Notre Dame No. 2 on the school's all-time list with 30 career touchdown grabs, behind only Michael Floyd (37), and is the only player in Irish history with back-to-back years with 14-plus receiving scores.

Fun Fact: Led the nation in receiving yards per catch (20.3) among pass-catchers with at least 55 receptions in 2015.

Ideal Team Fit: Although he will likely never be a true No. 1 target for a team, Fuller is a speed demon who can pull away from defensive backs, and all 32 teams have use for a dynamic talent like that.

NFL Comparison: Devin Smith

Speed kills. And there wasn't a better deep threat in college football the last few years than Will Fuller, who frequently took the top off the defense and drew coverage away from Notre Dame's other targets. After originally committing to Penn State, Fuller flipped to Notre Dame and red-shirted in 2012. He became a starter in 2014 as a sophomore and led the team with 76 receptions for 1,094 yards and 15 touchdowns (tying the single-season school record), earning All-America honors. He led the Irish in receiving again in 2015 as a junior, finishing with 62 catches for 1,258 yards and 14 touchdowns.

STRENGTHS: Galloping acceleration to reach top speed quickly and stretch the field vertically, stacking receivers and using multiple gears to pull away from defenders (averaged 20.3 yards per catch in 2015). Finds the ball well in flight with above-average tracking skills. Times his jumps to high-point and rarely misjudges downfield throws, working hard for body position to force defenders to go through him at the catch point. Achieves proper depth in his routes with the start/stop ability, change-of-direction skills, and hesitation to create separation at the stem. Shows a strong understanding of field leverage, pressing defenders and generating space. Hits the jets quickly to erase pursuit angles on inside screens. Scrappy, willing blocker. Experienced lining up outside and in the slot. Driven, hard-working, and has become a dependable practice player.

WEAKNESSES: Lean-muscled and lacks an ideal body type with below-average functional strength, allowing defenders to knock him off his route. Smaller hands and prone to body catches with too many drops on his college film. An equal-opportunity dropper, losing focus on various types of passes, including contested situations. Shows some indecision as a ball carrier and needs to get north-south quicker. Lacks the run power to pick up yards after initial contact. Bad habit of extending his arms downfield and pushing off, leading to penalties. Willing blocker, but struggles to sustain and limited in this area. Doesn't offer experience as a return man.

SUMMARY: A two-year starter in Notre Dame's power-spread offense, Fuller developed into the Irish's top playmaker the last two seasons, eclipsing 1,000 yards receiving both years and totaling 30 touchdowns in 29 career starts. A dynamic deep threat, Fuller has the uncanny ability to create separation late in his route, using an extra gear when the ball is in the air, a burst that most cornerbacks can't match. He is outstanding at tracking the deep ball and going and getting it, but the lapses in concentration and dropped passes are frustrating. Although NFL teams will need to look past his average build and streaky ball skills, Fuller is a big-time playmaker who has the speed to stretch the field and quickness to generate separation at the top of his routes.

CAREER STATS

SEASON	GP/GS	REC	REC YD	REC AVG	REC TD
2013	13/3	6	160	26.7	1
2014	13/13	76	1,094	14.4	15
2015	13/13	62	1,258	20.3	14
Career	39/29	144	2,512	17.4	30

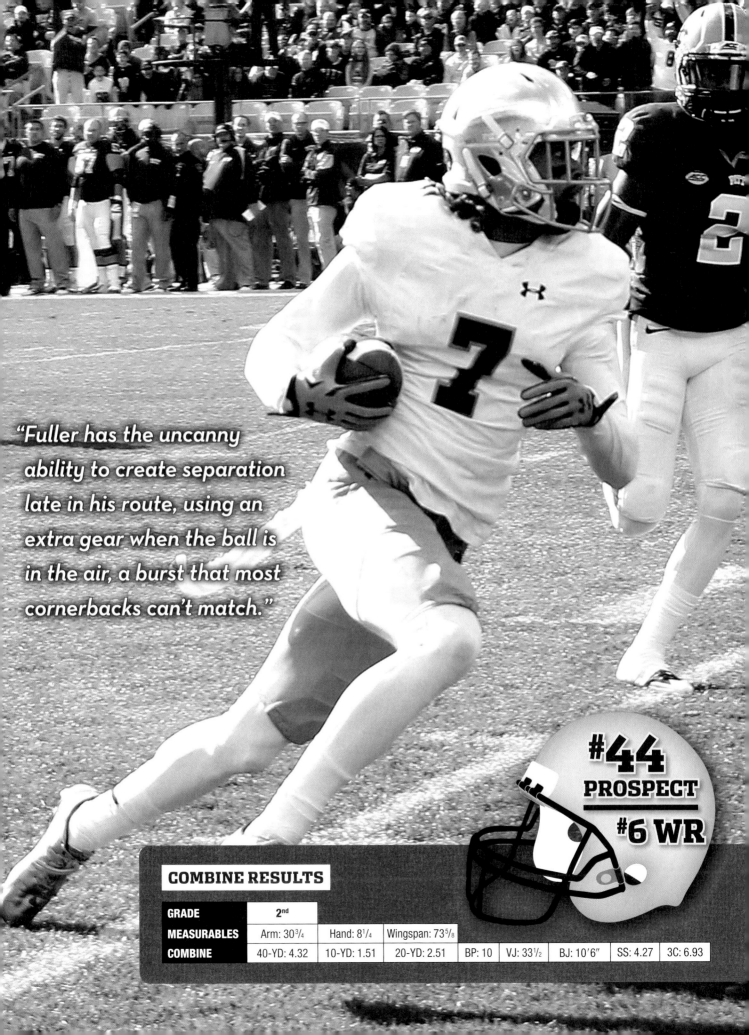

"Fuller has the uncanny ability to create separation late in his route, using an extra gear when the ball is in the air, a burst that most cornerbacks can't match."

#44 PROSPECT
#6 WR

COMBINE RESULTS

GRADE	2nd							
MEASURABLES	Arm: 30¾	Hand: 8¼	Wingspan: 73⅝					
COMBINE	40-YD: 4.32	10-YD: 1.51	20-YD: 2.51	BP: 10	VJ: 33½	BJ: 10'6"	SS: 4.27	3C: 6.93

DERRICK HENRY
RB / ALABAMA

Name: Derrick Henry

Ht: 6'2⅝" **Wt:** 247

Hometown/High School: Yulee, FL./Yulee

Class: Junior

Number: 2

DOB: July 17, 1994

Career Highlights: CFP National Champion (2016), Heisman Trophy (2015), Doak Walker Award (2015), Maxwell Award (2015), First-Team All-American (2015), First-Team All-SEC (2015)

Did You Know? Broke Tim Tebow's SEC record for consecutive games with at least one touchdown run, finding the end zone in 20 straight games.

Fun Fact: Set a new national high school record with 12,124 rushing yards in his career at Yulee High School, breaking Ken Hall's 51-year mark.

Ideal Team Fit: Best suited for a zone-blocking scheme where he can read, make one cut, and burst to the second level of the defense, using his strides and power to wear down the defense. He would be a natural fit for a team like the Dallas Cowboys, Houston Texans, or Seattle Seahawks.

NFL Comparison: Mix of Brandon Jacobs and LeGarrette Blount

Although he was Alabama's full-time starter for only one season, Derrick Henry leaves Tuscaloosa as the school's all-time leading rusher (3,591 yards), passing Shaun Alexander. He shared carries with T.J. Yeldon in 2014 before becoming the bell-cow featured runner for the Crimson Tide in 2015, breaking Herschel Walker's SEC rushing record with 2,219 yards and 28 touchdowns. His rushing total also led the FBS and won him numerous accolades, including the Heisman Trophy, Doak Walker Award, and Maxwell Award. Since 2011, Alabama has had four running backs drafted in the first two rounds. Henry should be the fifth.

STRENGTHS: Built like a linebacker with firm muscle tone and a physical body type. Not an easy ball carrier to finish off, as he is always falling forward, running with purpose and natural strength. Balanced and he continues to pump his legs after initial contact, using powerful body control and a long stiff-arm to keep defenders from his body. Displays strong strides and is able to stretch his legs and hit another gear at the second level. Shows vision and run anticipation to follow blocks and consistently make smart decisions. Attacks the line of scrimmage with conviction and doesn't need gaping run lanes, making himself skinny to clear holes. Adequate route runner and pass-catcher and showed improvements in pass protection as a blocker, squaring and anchoring to protect the pocket. Reliable ball security with only five career fumbles. Proven workhorse and wears down the defense, averaging 31.7 carries per game versus SEC competition in 2015. Humble, goal-oriented player who buys into coaching and expects the most out of himself.

WEAKNESSES: Taller than ideal for the position with long legs and high pad level, which presents a big target for defenders. Choppy footwork when forced to redirect, lacking ideal elusiveness or dynamic athleticism to create on his own. Tends to be sluggish and overly patient to the hole at times, taking too long to pick his lane, needing a runway to get started. Struggles to generate push when he doesn't lower his pads and isn't a traditional power back. Needs to eliminate the drops and improve his focus at the catch point. Took a lot of hits his final season in college, which might create lingering durability issues.

SUMMARY: Henry is a powerful, yet graceful north-south athlete who can fit through tight spaces, using patience and instincts to gash defenses. He is a runaway train who is tough to slow down once he gets going, and his final carry is as strong as his first—he gets better as the game progresses. He attacks downhill and pumps his legs with light feet, but his long legs and tall torso/pads aren't ideal. Henry will struggle to be as dominant in the NFL as he was at Alabama, but he has the athletic skill-set to be a tough, reliable grinder.

CAREER STATS

SEASON	GP/GS	RUSH ATT	RUSH YD	RUSH AVG	RUSH TD	REC	REC YD	REC AVG	REC TD
2013	12/0	35	382	10.9	3	1	61	61.0	1
2014	14/2	172	990	5.8	11	5	133	26.6	2
2015	15/15	395	2,219	5.6	28	11	91	8.3	0
Career	41/17	602	3,591	6.0	42	17	285	16.8	3

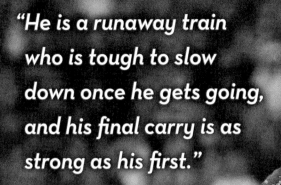

"He is a runaway train who is tough to slow down once he gets going, and his final carry is as strong as his first."

#45 PROSPECT

#2 RB

COMBINE RESULTS

GRADE	2nd							
MEASURABLES	Arm: 33	Hand: 8¾	Wingspan: 80¾					
COMBINE	40-YD: 4.54	10-YD: 1.60	20-YD: 2.67	BP: 22	VJ: 37	BJ: 10'10"	SS: 4.38	3C: 7.20

WILLIAM JACKSON III
CB / HOUSTON

Name: William Jackson III

Ht: 6'3⅜" **Wt:** 189

Hometown/High School: Houston, TX / Wheatley

Class: Senior

Number: 3

DOB: October 27, 1992

Career Highlights: Second-Team All-AAC (2015), Second-Team All-AAC (2014)

Did You Know? Led all of college football with 23 pass break-ups in 2015, which is the second-highest total the last 20 years, behind only Aqib Talib (28 in 2006).

Fun Fact: Turned into a playmaker with the ball in his hands following interceptions, averaging 26.4 yards per pickoff return, including three defensive touchdowns.

Ideal Team Fit: While his skill-set isn't an ideal fit for every scheme, Jackson is the type of long, physical corner who fits man-to-man coverages that teams like the Seattle Seahawks and Green Bay Packers favor.

NFL Comparison: Byron Maxwell

A Houston native, William Jackson was recruited by various schools around the country at both cornerback and receiver, but he chose to play his college ball close to home. After a season at Trinity Valley Community College to get his grades sorted out, Jackson saw his playing time increase throughout the 2013 season at Houston, becoming a full-time starter in 2014. He knocked on the NFL door as a junior before kicking it down as a senior with an NCAA-best 28 passes defended, leading the team with five interceptions in 2015.

STRENGTHS: Tall, smooth-muscled body type with a large wingspan. Above-average arm length for the position to expand his pass-defense radius and get his hands on the ball. Natural ball skills to high-point and disrupt the catch point. Speed to stay stride-for-stride down the field. Brackets receivers against the sideline to gain proper body position. Balanced off the snap and extends his hands to jam in press-man coverage. Quick out of his stance to shadow routes, reading the receiver to sense throws and get his head turned to react accordingly. Good plant-and-drive in off-coverage, showing timing to take away short passes or arrive at the same time as the ball. Physical finisher and shows the ability to wrap with his long arms and deliver a pop. Improved his focus at Houston, making appropriate changes to his preparation and study habits— became much more studious in the film room as a senior, and it showed.

WEAKNESSES: Leggy athlete and feet can get clunky in his transition. Quick to open his hips and bail, making it tough for him to redirect and attack underneath routes. Not silky smooth and shows hip tightness. Allows receivers to drive him off the pattern with hard stops. Needs to better anticipate routes and improve his spatial awareness to close gaps at the stem. Lacks a second gear to recover if the receiver gains a step vertically. Will panic and get grabby at times, attracting obvious penalties. Needs to better square up as a tackler. Too easily blocked for his size, needs to do more to stay free in the run game. Minor left knee injury (November 2015) that required a heavy brace.

SUMMARY: Jackson played mostly press and off-man coverage at Houston and would often shadow the opponents' top receiving threat, leaving school with a record 48 passes defended. A wideout and corner in high school, he does a lot of receiver-like things at the catch point, using his size, length, and ball skills to disrupt and be a playmaker. Jackson lacks the twitchy footwork or change-of-direction skills to easily redirect in short spaces, which will get him in trouble when he turns his hips and bails in off-coverages, but is much more comfortable in press-man when he can stay sticky to the receiver and use his back-to-the-ball awareness.

CAREER STATS

SEASON	GP/GS	TACKLES	TFL	SACKS	FF	PASS DEF	INT
2013	13/4	35	0.0	0.0	1	8	1
2014	13/12	37	1.5	0.0	1	12	2
2015	13/12	43	1.5	0.0	0	28	5
Career	39/28	115	3.0	0.0	2	48	8

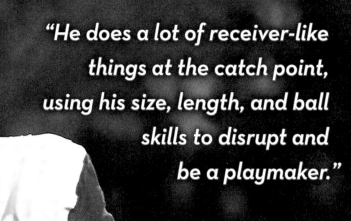

"He does a lot of receiver-like things at the catch point, using his size, length, and ball skills to disrupt and be a playmaker."

#46 PROSPECT

#5 CB

COMBINE RESULTS

GRADE	2nd							
MEASURABLES	Arm: 31¾	Hand: 9¼	Wingspan: 75¼					
COMBINE	40-YD: 4.37	10-YD: 1.52	20-YD: 2.56	BP: 10	VJ: —	BJ: 9′8″	SS: —	3C: —

LEONARD FLOYD
LB / GEORGIA

Name: Leonard Floyd

Ht: 6′5⅝″ **Wt:** 244

Hometown/High School: Eastman, GA / Dodge County

Class: Junior

Number: 84

DOB: September 8, 1992

Career Highlights: Second-Team All-SEC (2015), All-American (2015), Georgia Defensive MVP (2014), Freshman All-SEC (2013)

Did You Know? Spent the 2012 season at Hargrave Military Academy after not qualifying out of high school due to an online course that wasn't accepted.

Fun Fact: The day Mark Richt was fired as Georgia's head coach, Floyd tweeted that he was leaving for the NFL, posting, "Coach Richt probably was the only one that could have convinced me to stay."

Ideal Team Fit: One of the best athletes in the 2016 draft class, Floyd will need protection in the NFL due to his lack of core strength and is ideally suited as an off-ball linebacker and sub-package rusher in a 3-4 scheme.

NFL Comparison: Barkevious Mingo

A versatile front-seven defender, Leonard Floyd has the silky-smooth athleticism that allowed Georgia to mix and match him based on the opponent and situation. Growing up in rural Georgia, he committed to the Bulldogs very early and stuck to his pledge over offers from Alabama, Florida, and others. Floyd started eight games in 2013 and earned Freshman All-SEC honors, recording a team-best 6.5 sacks. He started 11 games as a sophomore and was voted team defensive MVP with 55 tackles, 8.5 tackles for loss, and six sacks. He had his best season in 2015 as a junior, leading the team in tackles for loss (10.5) and sacks (4.5) to make second-team All-SEC.

STRENGTHS: Tall frame with long arms and room to add weight. Above-average athleticism with excellent movement skills and long-striding pursuit speed. Screams off the edge and looks like a track athlete bending, staying low, and flattening his path to the quarterback. Natural agility to make quick cuts to avoid contact, cross the face of blockers, and knife through gaps. Very good chase range with the loose hips to stick with receivers in coverage. Improved awareness against the run to hold contain and string runs to the sideline. Active arms to keep blockers busy. Versatile starting experience, splitting his snaps at inside and outside linebacker and at the hybrid "STAR" position in nickel packages. Doesn't take plays off and genuinely loves playing the game.

WEAKNESSES: Lean bone structure with twig limbs, thin torso, and concerns about how much weight he can add—looks like A.J. Green in his Georgia uniform, which isn't a positive quality for a pass rusher. Below average functional strength, struggling to generate movement at the point of attack or convert speed to power. Too easily controlled on the edges and can be eliminated when he doesn't effectively use his length. Core strength issues, struggling to maintain his balance through contact. Needs to develop his hand tactics and pass-rush arsenal. Long arms to obstruct passing lanes, but lacks the awareness to take advantage in this area. Football instincts are still in the development phase. History of shoulder issues.

SUMMARY: A three-year starter, Floyd lined up mostly at strong-side linebacker in Georgia's 3-4 base, but also filled in at inside linebacker and at hybrid "STAR," dropping into coverage. Highly intriguing with his size/length/athleticism, he shows the impressive rush skills to stab, dip, and flatten around the edge like a heat-seeking missile, maintaining his balance without losing speed to the pocket. Floyd is deadly in space, but his lack of functional strength and growth potential are glaring concerns—once blockers make contact, he's usually shut down. His coaches rave about his natural ability and selfless versatility, plugging him in at different spots in the front seven, which helps his NFL transition.

CAREER STATS

SEASON	GP/GS	TACKLES	TFL	SACKS	FF	INT
2013	13/8	55	9.5	6.5	2	0
2014	12/11	55	8.5	6.0	3	0
2015	13/13	74	10.5	4.5	0	0
Career	38/32	184	28.5	17.0	5	0

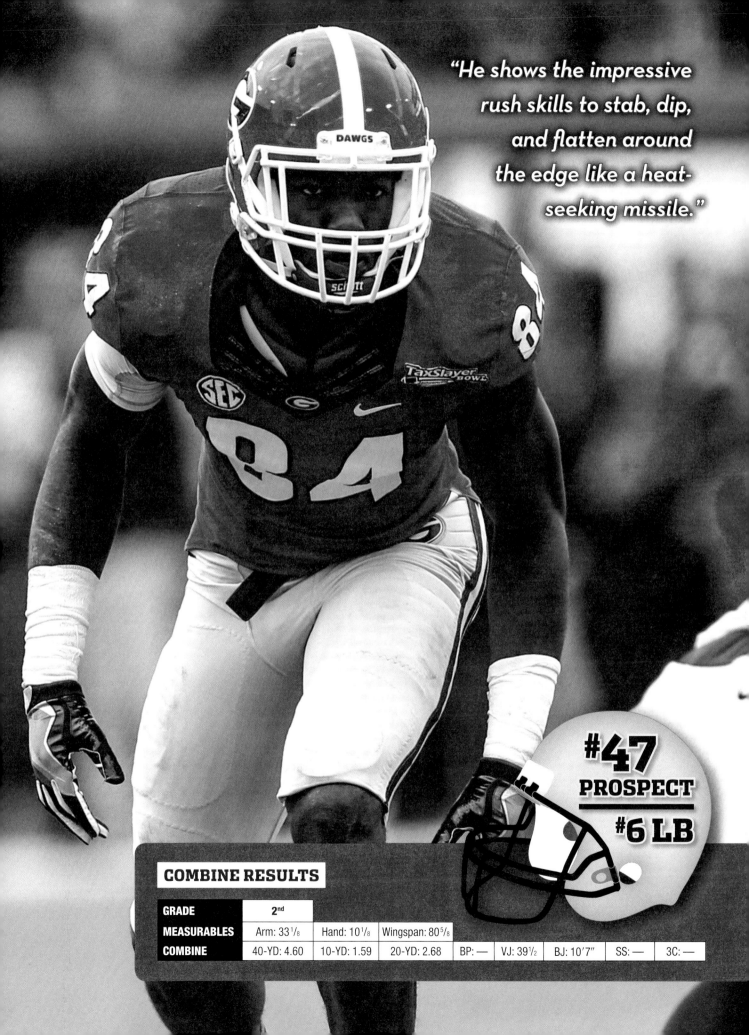

"He shows the impressive rush skills to stab, dip, and flatten around the edge like a heat-seeking missile."

#47 PROSPECT

#6 LB

COMBINE RESULTS

GRADE	2nd							
MEASURABLES	Arm: 33 1/8	Hand: 10 1/8	Wingspan: 80 5/8					
COMBINE	40-YD: 4.60	10-YD: 1.59	20-YD: 2.68	BP: —	VJ: 39 1/2	BJ: 10'7"	SS: —	3C: —

JOSH DOCTSON
WR / TCU

Name: Josh Doctson

Ht: 6′2″ **Wt:** 202

Hometown/High School: Mansfield, TX / Legacy

Class: Redshirt Senior

Number: 9

DOB: December 3, 1992

Career Highlights: First-Team All–Big 12 (2015), First-Team All-American (2015), Finalist for the Biletnikoff Award (2015), Second-Team All–Big 12 honors (2014)

Did You Know? Holds the Horned Frogs records for most receiving yards in school history (2,785) and in a single game (267)—only three times in TCU's history has a player gone over 1,000 yards receiving in a season, and twice it was Doctson.

Fun Fact: Was part of the TCU "Bleacher Creature" tradition when he was 10 years old, running onto the field at Amon G. Carter Stadium each week before kickoff.

Ideal Team Fit: Has the ability to make an inaccurate quarterback look consistent due to his large catch radius down the field. He has the vertical prowess to carve out a niche in an offense that routinely tests defenses through the air like the Atlanta Falcons or New York Giants.

NFL Comparison: Jordan Matthews

From walk-on to All-American, Josh Doctson started his career at Wyoming, but due to an illness in his family, he sought a transfer closer to home, walking on at TCU (his childhood dream school). After sitting out the 2012 season, he worked his way into the starting rotation at receiver as a sophomore and led the team in receiving with 36 catches for 440 yards and four touchdowns. Doctson emerged as one of the better wide receivers in the country as a junior in 2014, but had his best season in 2015 as a senior, setting new TCU records for receptions (79), receiving yards (1,327), and touchdown catches (14), in only 10 games.

STRENGTHS: Tall athlete with long arms and adequate muscle tone for the position. Shows outstanding leaping ability, body control, and ball skills to elevate and out-jump defenders. Twists his frame and extends with magnet hands to pluck away from his body, displaying terrific focus and tracking ability. Attacks the ball, doesn't wait for it to come to him. Uses his body well to box out and shield defenders from the ball. Immediately looks to turn catches downfield with deceiving run toughness and a strong stiff arm. Creates spacing in his routes and finds open zones to give his quarterback a clear target. Unselfish, dependable, and hungry worker, making it tough to find anyone who will say a negative word about him. Highly productive, leading TCU in receiving each of his three seasons with the program.

WEAKNESSES: Lean-framed and thin-boned, limiting his growth potential. Upright runner and won't break many tackles as a ball carrier, running tough, but not powerful. Tentative versus press and over the middle, looking for the safety and not attacking the ball with the same vigor. Will have some drops, allowing footsteps to distract him at the catch point. Not a proficient route runner at this stage in his development—not below average in this area, but still has a lot of room to grow. Doesn't offer any return experience on special teams. Coming off a wrist injury (November 2015) that prematurely ended his TCU career.

SUMMARY: A three-year starter in TCU's spread offense, Doctson blossomed at flanker when Gary Patterson hired offensive coordinators Sonny Cumbie and Doug Meacham prior to the 2014 season to inject life into the play-calling. All of his experience came in a spread offense that didn't ask him to run a full route tree, but he shows outstanding effort on throws in his zip code. Doctson has the remarkable ability to expand his catch radius and contort his body, finding ways to bail out erratic throws and finish catches. Doctson lacks polish in areas, but has the resilient mentality and on-field skill-set to contribute early and settle into a No. 2 receiver role.

CAREER STATS

SEASON	GP/GS	REC	REC YD	REC AVG	REC TD
2011	12/9	35	393	11.2	5
2013	12/6	36	440	12.2	4
2014	13/12	65	1,018	15.7	11
2015	10/10	79	1,327	16.8	14
Career	47/37	215	3,178	14.8	34

"Doctson has the remarkable ability to expand his catch radius and contort his body, finding ways to bail out erratic throws and finish catches."

#48 PROSPECT

#7 WR

COMBINE RESULTS

GRADE	2nd							
MEASURABLES	Arm: 31⁷⁄₈	Hand: 9⁷⁄₈	Wingspan: 76⁵⁄₈					
COMBINE	40-YD: 4.50	10-YD: 1.58	20-YD: 2.62	BP: 14	VJ: 41	BJ: 10'11"	SS: 4.08	3C: 6.84

BRAXTON MILLER
WR / OHIO STATE

Name: Braxton Miller

Ht: 6′1⅜″ **Wt:** 201

Hometown/High School:
Huber Heights, OH / Wayne

Class: Redshirt Senior **Number:** 1

DOB: May 26, 1992

Career Highlights: Senior Bowl (2016), CFP National Champion (2015), Big Ten Offensive Player of the Year (2013), Griese-Brees Big Ten Quarterback of the Year (2013), Big Ten Offensive Player of the Year (2012), Griese-Brees Big Ten Quarterback of the Year (2012)

Did You Know? One of only six players in Ohio State history to rush for 3,300 yards over his career, joining Archie Griffin, Ezekiel Elliott, Eddie George, Tim Spencer, and Beanie Wells.

Fun Fact: Has the Ohio State logo (block "O") tattooed on his left shoulder. He had the ink done more than a week prior to his official commitment to the Buckeyes and had to wear long sleeves until he made the announcement formal.

Ideal Team Fit: Due to his raw traits as a receiver, Miller enters the NFL as more of a project than polished wideout, but he's a special athlete with considerable upside. He will likely be used as a gadget player as a rookie before competing for a starting receiver role in year two.

NFL Comparison: A faster Julian Edelman

One of the most exciting athletes at the college level in recent years, Braxton Miller was a two-time Big Ten Offensive Player of the Year at quarterback, and the stage was set for a special senior season in 2014. However, the football gods had different plans as he injured his right (throwing) shoulder in the 2013 Orange Bowl and then reinjured the same shoulder the following summer, tearing his labrum and requiring surgery. The injury forced Miller to redshirt in 2014 and change positions, returning for the 2015 season as a hybrid H-Back. He caught a pass in 12 of 13 games last season and finished third on the team with 26 receptions for 341 yards and three touchdowns.

STRENGTHS: Athletic body type and solidly built for the position. Possesses extraordinary athleticism and speed with sudden, explosive cutting ability. Tremendous balance and body control in all of his movements with multiple gears to separate in his routes and as a ball carrier. Understands hesitation in his patterns, setting up defenders before bursting in different directions. Vision to be a big play threat whenever he touches the ball. Shows the locating ability and reflexes to track and keep his focus through the catch. Deceiving body strength to squirm out of would-be tackles. Strong-armed passer and spins a pretty ball, bringing versatility to offensive play-callers. Mature leader who wants to be great.

WEAKNESSES: Raw route runner and lacks experience at the receiver position. Needs to improve his footwork, especially at the stem of patterns, using too many steps. Natural hands, but had some drops in 2015, especially when receiving fastballs. Still learning how to properly adjust to throws and attack at the highest point. Shows alligator arms and tends to be too concerned with what's going on around him, bracing for contact and being tentative over the middle. Constantly looking for the home run, leading to too much east-west in his movements. Ball security needs tightening with 30 career fumbles (three fumbles in 2015 as a non-quarterback). Minimal special teams experience. Health is an obvious concern with his past medical issues.

SUMMARY: A former quarterback, Miller's 2014 shoulder surgery ended up being a blessing in disguise, allowing him to speed up the inevitable transition to a skill position for the next level. Miller is a gifted and exciting open-field athlete with game-changing speed and the twitched-up ability to be elusive, not slowing down in his cuts. He is able to translate his ability to read defenses as a passer to reading coverages in his routes, but is still unpolished in this area and will need time as he continues his development at wide receiver. The No. 1 concern moving forward for Miller is durability—a true competitor, but can he stay healthy?

CAREER STATS

SEASON	GP/GS	RUSH ATT	RUSH YD	RUSH AVG	RUSH TD	REC	REC YD	REC AVG	REC TD
2011	12/10	159	715	4.5	7	0	0	0.0	0
2012	12/12	227	1,271	5.6	13	0	0	0.0	0
2013	12/12	171	1,068	6.2	12	0	0	0.0	0
2015	13/7	42	260	6.2	1	26	341	13.1	3
Career	49/41	599	3,314	5.5	33	26	341	13.1	3

"Miller is a gifted and exciting open-field athlete with game-changing speed and the twitched-up ability to be elusive."

#49 PROSPECT

#8 WR

COMBINE RESULTS

GRADE	2nd							
MEASURABLES	Arm: 31¾	Hand: 9⅛	Wingspan: 74					
COMBINE	40-YD: 4.50	10-YD: 1.60	20-YD: 2.66	BP: 17	VJ: 35	BJ: 10'3"	SS: 4.07	3C: 6.65

ARTIE BURNS
CB / MIAMI (FL)

Name: Artie Burns

Ht: 5'11⁷/₈" **Wt:** 193

Hometown/High School: Miami, FL / Miami Northwestern

Class: Junior

Number: 1

DOB: May 1, 1995

Career Highlights: Second-Team All-ACC (2015)

Did You Know? In the days following the death of Artie's mother last October, Miami set up a GoFundMe page and helped raise over $35,000 in the first 24 hours to assist in funeral expenses.

Fun Fact: Like his mother, Burns was a standout track athlete and set several high school records, including in the 110-meter hurdles (13.35) and 300-meter hurdles (36.14).

Ideal Team Fit: Although he might not be a full-time starter until year two, Burns has the athletic ingredients to be a physical press corner in the NFL, fitting a team like the Kansas City Chiefs.

NFL Comparison: Jalen Collins

With offers from USC, LSU, and other top schools around the country, Artie Burns had options out of high school, but chose to stay home and become a Hurricane. After seeing most of his playing time on special teams as a true freshman, he became a starter in 2014 as a sophomore and recorded 40 tackles and six passes defended. Burns had his most productive season in 2015 as a junior, starting 12 games and leading the ACC in interceptions (six) to earn second-team All-ACC honors. Due to his mother's sudden death (heart attack) and his father currently serving a 25-year prison sentence (cocaine trafficking), Burns has custody of his two younger brothers and his son, citing his family as the reason for his early jump to the NFL.

STRENGTHS: Good-sized athlete for the position with excellent height, length, and growth potential. Above-average play speed with the transitional quickness, hips, and body control to ride routes downfield. Great adjustments on the ball in flight to aggressively locate and attack—wants the ball more than receivers. Crowds the catch point and doesn't allow receivers to get comfortable. Strong hands to jam and reroute in press. Stings in run support, breaking down in space to wrap and wrestle. Bat out of hell as a blitzer, closing with an extra gear. Ball skills to finish interceptions—his six interceptions in 2015 was the most by a Hurricanes player since 2004 first-round pick Sean Taylor. Experienced on special teams coverages. Focuses on the details with the mental toughness to work through adversity.

WEAKNESSES: Lean limbs and needs to continue and add bulk to his frame. Struggles to shed blocks and needs to develop his functional strength. Tenacious tackler, but hugs too much, and his tackle attempts require mechanical refinement. Will turn his hips too early off the snap and needs to improve his transitional sink. Panics after a false step, grabbing to slow down the receiver and attracting penalties. Can be driven off patterns and be late to recover versus comeback routes. Needs to develop his eye discipline and spatial awareness, allowing receivers to get vertical and create spacing.

SUMMARY: A two-year starter for the Hurricanes, Burns played primarily at boundary cornerback at Miami, starting 23 games the last two seasons. Play speed at the cornerback position is critical for the next level, and he checks that box with the lower body explosion and hip fluidity to play tight coverage in both man and zone coverages. Burns has receiver-like traits to limit passing windows, but needs to better anticipate routes and cut down on the holding downfield. Although undisciplined as a tackler and with his hands in coverage, Burns has the requisite play speed, competitive toughness, and budding ball awareness to develop into a starting press corner in the NFL.

CAREER STATS

SEASON	GP/GS	TACKLES	TFL	SACKS	FF	PASS DEF	INT
2013	11/0	17	0.5	0.0	1	4	1
2014	13/11	40	2.0	2.0	0	6	0
2015	13/12	39	0.5	0.0	0	13	6
Career	37/23	96	3.0	2.0	1	23	7

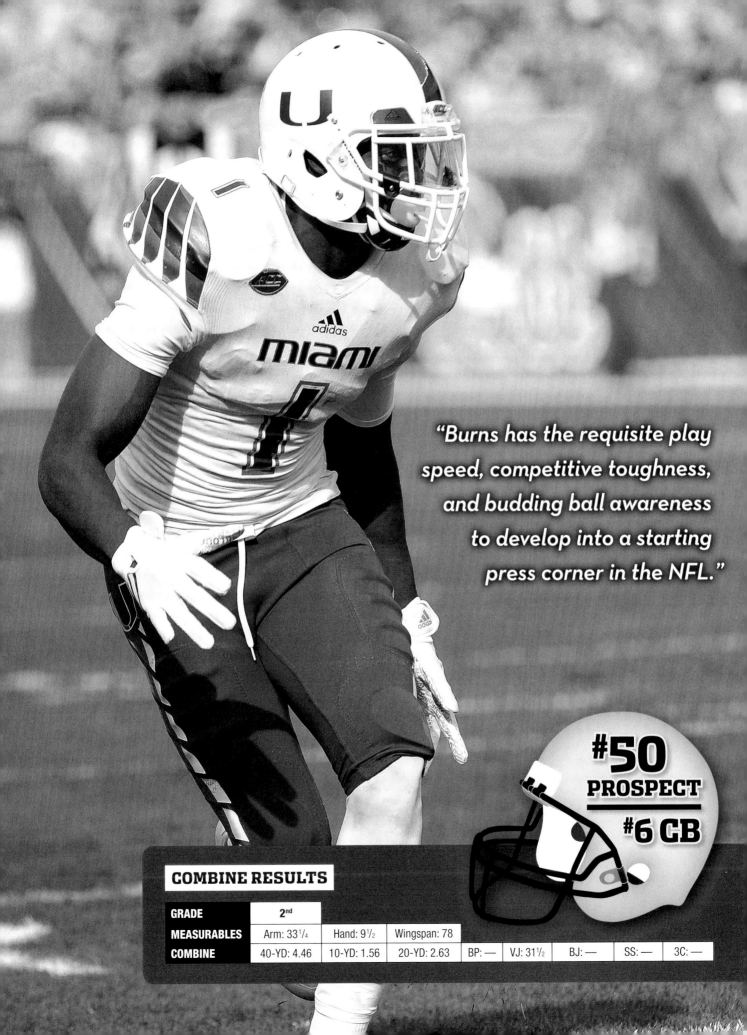

"Burns has the requisite play speed, competitive toughness, and budding ball awareness to develop into a starting press corner in the NFL."

#50 PROSPECT
#6 CB

COMBINE RESULTS

GRADE	2nd							
MEASURABLES	Arm: 33¼	Hand: 9½	Wingspan: 78					
COMBINE	40-YD: 4.46	10-YD: 1.56	20-YD: 2.63	BP: —	VJ: 31½	BJ: —	SS: —	3C: —

TYLER BOYD
WR / PITTSBURGH

Name: Tyler Boyd

Ht: 6'1½" **Wt:** 197

Hometown/High School: Clairton, PA / Clairton

Class: Junior

Number: 23

DOB: November 15, 1994

Career Highlights: First-Team All-ACC (2015), First-Team All-ACC (2014), Freshman All-American (2013)

Did You Know? First player in ACC history to tally 1,000-yard receiving seasons as both a freshman and sophomore.

Fun Fact: His 5,243 all-purpose yards are second-best in Pitt history, behind only Pro and College Hall of Famer Tony Dorsett.

Ideal Team Fit: With his quick hands and sharp route-running, Boyd would be an ideal fit in the slot, similar to the way the Miami Dolphins utilize Jarvis Landry.

NFL Comparison: Keenan Allen

Larry Fitzgerald is the greatest receiver to come out of the Pitt program, but the most prolific? That distinction belongs to Tyler Boyd, the school leader in career receptions (254), receiving yards (3,361), and several other receiving categories. He saw early playing time as a true freshman and set a new ACC freshman record with 85 receptions and 1,174 receiving yards, breaking Fitzgerald's freshman records in both categories. Boyd set career bests in receiving yards (1,261) as a sophomore and in catches (91) as a junior, and was the lone unanimous first-team player on the All-ACC team in 2015.

STRENGTHS: Gliding athlete with an instant accelerator to reach his top speed with his initial strides. Shows sharp cuts and burst off his plant foot, mixing gears in his patterns. Quick release off the line with natural route running prowess, setting up defenders and selling patterns with beautiful body fakes. Easy body control to twist in midair and adjust to obscure ball placement. Excellent hand-eye coordination with strong hands to pluck, extending his catching radius beyond what most his size can—attacks the ball, doesn't wait for it. Lack of body strength shows in traffic, but he is surprisingly efficient in contested situations. Tough over the middle and always looking to pick up yards after the catch with innate field awareness. Highly competitive playing temperament and is known as a lunch-pail worker. Lined up everywhere in the Pitt offense, including outside, slot, and in the backfield. Boyd was also a return man on Pitt special teams, averaging 24.4 yards on kickoff returns and 8.8 yards on punt returns.

WEAKNESSES: Underwhelming size with a thin torso, lean body features, and limited bulk. Doesn't have the power to fight through tackle attempts or routinely pick up yards after initial contact, lacking the ideal build to take consistent punishment in the NFL. Majority of his routes at Pitt were within seven yards of the line of scrimmage (screens, slants, etc.), and he is unproven as a consistent downfield threat. Feels ghosts around him, leading to focus drops. Holds the ball too loose as a ball carrier, leading to ball security concerns. Struggles to gain correct positioning as a blocker with below-average functional strength, lacking the refined technique to compensate. Off-field decision-making needs investigation after a DUI arrest (June 2015), leading to a one-game suspension.

SUMMARY: A three-year starter, Boyd played with three different starting QBs each of his three years with the Panthers, but his production was consistent each season, leaving Pitt as the school's all-time leading receiver. A graceful athlete, he trusts his hands and uses quick eyes to snatch and immediately analyze his surroundings, but his body size does lead to durability concerns, especially over the middle. Despite average measurables, Boyd is an exquisite catcher of the football and able to stand out by paying attention to the details.

CAREER STATS

SEASON	GP/GS	REC	REC YD	REC AVG	REC TD
2013	13/10	85	1,174	13.8	7
2014	13/12	78	1,261	16.2	8
2015	12/12	91	926	10.2	6
Career	38/34	254	3,361	13.2	21

"Despite only average measurables, Boyd is an exquisite catcher of the football and able to stand out by paying attention to the details."

#51 PROSPECT

#9 WR

COMBINE RESULTS

GRADE	2nd							
MEASURABLES	Arm: 32	Hand: 9¾	Wingspan: 76⅜					
COMBINE	40-YD: 4.58	10-YD: 1.59	20-YD: 2.66	BP: 11	VJ: 34	BJ: 9'11"	SS: 4.35	3C: 6.90

SHON COLEMAN
OT / AUBURN

Name: Shon Coleman

Ht: 6'5½" **Wt:** 307

Hometown/High School: Memphis, TN / Olive Branch

Class: Redshirt Junior

Number: 72

DOB: November 25, 1991

Career Highlights: Second-Team All-SEC (2015)

Did You Know? Although his 30 months of chemo treatments kept him off the field, Coleman was still active in the classroom, earning his bachelor's and master's degrees at Auburn.

Fun Fact: Coleman is no stranger to walking across the stage during the NFL Draft, as he received the opportunity to announce the 14th overall selection in the 2014 NFL Draft at Radio City Music Hall (DT Aaron Donald to the Rams).

Ideal Team Fit: Although he requires time to develop once drafted, the ingredients and upside are there for Coleman to start in the NFL at offensive tackle for a long time.

NFL Comparison: A less-athletic Greg Robinson

CAREER STATS

SEASON	GP/GS	POS
2010	Sat out season	
2011	Sat out season	
2012	Redshirted	
2013	8/0	
2014	13/13	LT
2015	12/12	LT
Career	33/25	LT

The most interesting aspect of the NFL Draft process is learning the journey each player takes to arrive at this juncture. Shon Coleman has a story unlike any other. A highly touted, five-star recruit out of high school, Coleman committed to Auburn over offers from Alabama, Arkansas, and LSU. However, he was diagnosed with acute lymphoblastic leukemia in the spring of 2010 and spent the next two seasons focusing on the illness. After being declared cancer free, Coleman redshirted in 2012 as he worked to get back into football shape and spent the 2013 season as the backup to future first-round pick Greg Robinson. With Robinson off to the NFL, Coleman took over the left tackle job in 2014 and started 25 games the last two seasons, steadily progressing into one of the SEC's top blockers.

STRENGTHS: Looks the part with a wide-hipped, broad-shouldered frame. Flexible lower body to stay balanced even when overextended. Comfortable in space and nimble on his feet to pitch a tent at the second level. Not easily moved in pass protection or put in reverse. Extends well and has shock absorbers for arms, halting momentum generated by pass rushers. Quick punch and recoil, always keeping busy. Heavy hands with a strong upper body drive block. Competes like a bully and plays a physical brand of football. Highly determined and has handled inconceivable adversity, beating cancer and working his way back onto the football field.

WEAKNESSES: Still developing the bulk and muscle tone on his body. Bad habit of not moving his feet once engaged, falling off blocks. Needs to consistently bring his feet with him to avoid lunging with his upper body. Doesn't consistently utilize body angles in the run game. Strong hands at the point of attack, but needs to do a better job steering and redirecting defenders with those hands instead of just jolting. Active with his length, but the timing of his punches needs to be tweaked. Older (will be a 25-year-old NFL rookie). Medical evaluations are paramount to his draft grade due to his past battle with cancer.

SUMMARY: A two-year starting left tackle in Auburn's spread scheme, Coleman arrived at Auburn in 2010 as a top recruit with a chance to earn a starting job as a true freshman. But after a cancer diagnosis and the long road to recovery, Coleman worked his way back onto the field. He is a balanced big man with long arms, strong hands, and the mental and physical toughness that has been profoundly tested. But after spending three years away from the field, Coleman is still raw in several areas, bending too much at the waist and not properly using angles. Coleman has NFL starting potential if given time to develop, but the medical evaluations will be the deciding factor in his draft projection.

"Coleman is a balanced big man with long arms, strong hands, and the mental and physical toughness that has been profoundly tested."

#52 PROSPECT

#5 OT

COMBINE RESULTS

GRADE	2nd							
MEASURABLES	Arm: 35 1/8	Hand: 10 5/8	Wingspan: 83 1/2					
COMBINE	40-YD: —	10-YD: —	20-YD: —	BP: 22	VJ: —	BJ: —	SS: —	3C: —

JEREMY CASH
S / DUKE

Name: Jeremy Cash

Ht: 6′3⁄8″ **Wt:** 212

Hometown/High School: Miami, FL / Plantation

Class: Redshirt Senior

Number: 16

DOB: December 9, 1992

Career Highlights: ACC Defensive Player of the Year (2015), 2015 Consensus All-American (2015), Jim Thorpe Award Finalist (2015), First-Team All-ACC (2015), Second-Team All-American (2014), Second-Team All-ACC (2014), Second-Team All-American (2013), Second-Team All-ACC (2013)

Did You Know? If drafted in one of the top three rounds, Cash will be the first Blue Devils defensive prospect drafted in the top 100 picks since 1987.

Fun Fact: A self-described adrenaline junkie, Cash earned his psychology degree and hopes to work for the FBI one day.

Ideal Team Fit: Cash would thrive in a similar role as Arizona Cardinals hybrid safety/linebacker Deone Bucannon, an instinctive run defender who is always hunting near the line of scrimmage.

NFL Comparison: Deone Bucannon

Jeremy Cash began his career at Ohio State because of a bond he created with Jim Tressel, but he never had the opportunity to play for him. He decided to transfer when Urban Meyer was hired, saying he "definitely didn't see eye to eye" with the Buckeyes' new head coach. Based on a recommendation by Tressel, Cash landed at Duke to play for head coach David Cutcliffe, where he blossomed into one of the best defensive backs in the country, recording 100-plus tackles each of the last three seasons. He had his most productive season as a senior with a team-best 18 tackles for loss, becoming the first player in school history to earn All-America honors three straight years.

STRENGTHS: Adequate body type for the position with solid muscle definition. Smooth athlete with a quick first step and closing burst as a tackler. Lacks elite speed, but he doesn't play hesitant, so his play speed is better than his timed speed. Instinctive with a quick mental processor to recognize and see things before they happen, making him tough to block. Breaks down well in space with strong hands and accurate strike zone to finish tackles, leading with his shoulder. Leverages blocks and has excellent field awareness to force the action back inside. Shows very good timing at the line of scrimmage to shoot gaps and disrupt the backfield. Nonstop hustler as a run defender and routinely cleans up his teammates' messes due to effort and pursuit quickness. Highly intelligent on and off the field and is the unquestioned leader on defense, demanding excellence from his teammates with unforced bravado.

WEAKNESSES: Not an explosive athlete and lacks twitch in his movements. Has some hip stiffness with average-at-best long speed. Wasn't asked to pedal in college and needs to improve his transitional footwork to sink, turn, and stick with receivers, lacking experience playing in reverse. Can be overaggressive at times, overpursuing angles or jumping offside. Does his best work near the line of scrimmage and needs to become a better playmaker downfield.

SUMMARY: A three-year starter, Cash lined up as the starting "strike" safety in Duke's 4-2-5 base defense, a linebacker/safety hybrid position often lined up over the slot and near the line of scrimmage. His best attributes are his accurate first step and ability to recognize things quickly against the run, anticipating and showing terrific reaction quickness. Cash enjoys contact and understands football geometry, taking the most efficient path to the ball carrier. He was adequate in coverage on film, but also unproven down the seam and vertically. Cash wasn't asked to play in reverse at Duke, spending most of his time near the line of scrimmage, so NFL teams need to have a plan for his skill-set.

CAREER STATS

SEASON	GP/GS	TACKLES	TFL	SACKS	FF	PASS DEF	INT
2011	5/0	3	0.0	0.0	0	0	0
2013	14/14	121	9.5	0.0	2	8	4
2014	13/13	111	10.5	5.5	4	9	2
2015	12/12	101	18.0	2.5	3	4	0
Career	44/39	336	38.0	8.0	9	21	6

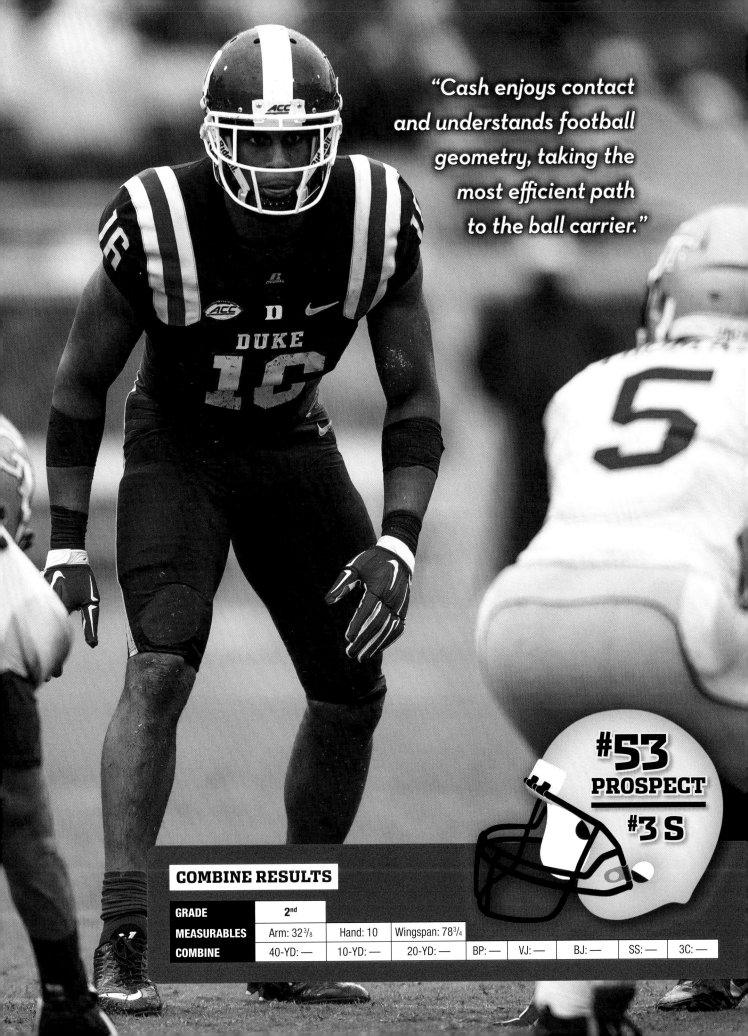

"Cash enjoys contact and understands football geometry, taking the most efficient path to the ball carrier."

#53
PROSPECT
#3 S

COMBINE RESULTS

GRADE	2nd							
MEASURABLES	Arm: 32 3/8	Hand: 10	Wingspan: 78 3/4					
COMBINE	40-YD: —	10-YD: —	20-YD: —	BP: —	VJ: —	BJ: —	SS: —	3C: —

CONNOR COOK
QB / MICHIGAN STATE

Name: Connor Cook

Ht: 6'4" **Wt:** 217

Hometown/High School: Hinckley, OH / Walsh Jesuit

Class: Redshirt Senior

Number: 18

DOB: January 29, 1993

Career Highlights: Griese-Brees Big Ten Quarterback of the Year Award (2015), First-Team All–Big Ten (2015), Second-Team All–Big Ten (2014), Second-Team All–Big Ten (2013)

Did You Know? Once drafted, Cook will be the fourth quarterback from Michigan State who will be active in the NFL, joining Kirk Cousins, Drew Stanton, and Brian Hoyer.

Fun Fact: Comes from an athletic family as his father (Chris) lettered at tight end at Indiana and mother (Donna) played basketball at Cincinnati.

Ideal Team Fit: Of all the quarterbacks in this draft class, Cook is the most ready to play as a rookie with his experience in a pro-style offense, but ideally needs an established No. 1 target and an offense committed to run/pass balance like the Houston Texans.

NFL Comparison: A less-athletic Ryan Tannehill

One of the Big Ten's top passers in recent memory, Connor Cook leaves Michigan State as the school's all-time winningest quarterback with a 34–5 career record. He won the starting quarterback job as a sophomore and posted consistent production each of his last three years, setting school records for career touchdown passes (71) and total offense (9,217). Cook became the first Michigan State quarterback to earn back-to-back all-conference honors in 2013 and 2014 and was named the Griese-Brees Big Ten Quarterback of the Year in 2015.

STRENGTHS: Good-sized athlete for the position with a solidly built frame to bounce back after hits and deliver some of his own on short-yardage runs. Above-average arm strength to deliver ropes, adding extra zip when able to step into his throws. Efficient delivery to get the ball out quickly with fast eyes to scan the field and work through progressions. Effective on-the-move passer with velocity and accuracy, and although he isn't a consistent rush threat, he has adequate foot quickness to escape the pocket and extend plays. Confident thrower and loves one-on-one matchups, putting the ball where his receiver can attack, trusting his teammates to make plays. Understands touch and controls his ball speeds well. A resilient competitor with a short memory on the field, rarely getting too high or low.

WEAKNESSES: Flawed footwork, often resting on his back foot and "arming" throws instead of using proper mechanics. Inconsistent body rhythm, weight transfer and base, especially when moved from his original spot, leading to accuracy issues. Never finished a season with his completion percentage above 59%. Needs to speed up his process and recognize passing windows have a limited expiration date. Streaky decision-maker and too willing to deliver into high-traffic coverage, stubbornly locking onto his initial read. Can be distracted by pressure and not poised in a muddy pocket, allowing his eye level to wander. Not a vocal player and wasn't voted a team captain as a senior, leading to questions about his ability to acclimate himself in an NFL locker room. His throwing (right) shoulder needs to be medically cleared after an injury (November 2015) that forced him to miss one game.

SUMMARY: A three-year starter in the Spartans' pro-style offense, Cook's résumé tape shows a tough, confident passer who will stand in the face of pressure and deliver NFL-style throws, doing a great job finding the one-on-one matchups and giving his target a chance to make a play. With a clean pocket, Cook has all the ingredients for the next level, but his game has holes outside of structure. Overall, Cook can start in the NFL as a rookie, but doesn't have a high ceiling and will need a strong supporting cast to be productive.

CAREER STATS

SEASON	GP/GS	CMP	ATT	PCT	YDS	TDS	INT
2012	3/0	9	17	52.9	94	1	1
2013	14/13	223	380	58.7	2,755	22	6
2014	13/13	212	365	58.1	3,214	24	8
2015	13/13	229	408	56.1	3,131	24	7
Career	43/39	673	1,170	57.5	9,194	71	22

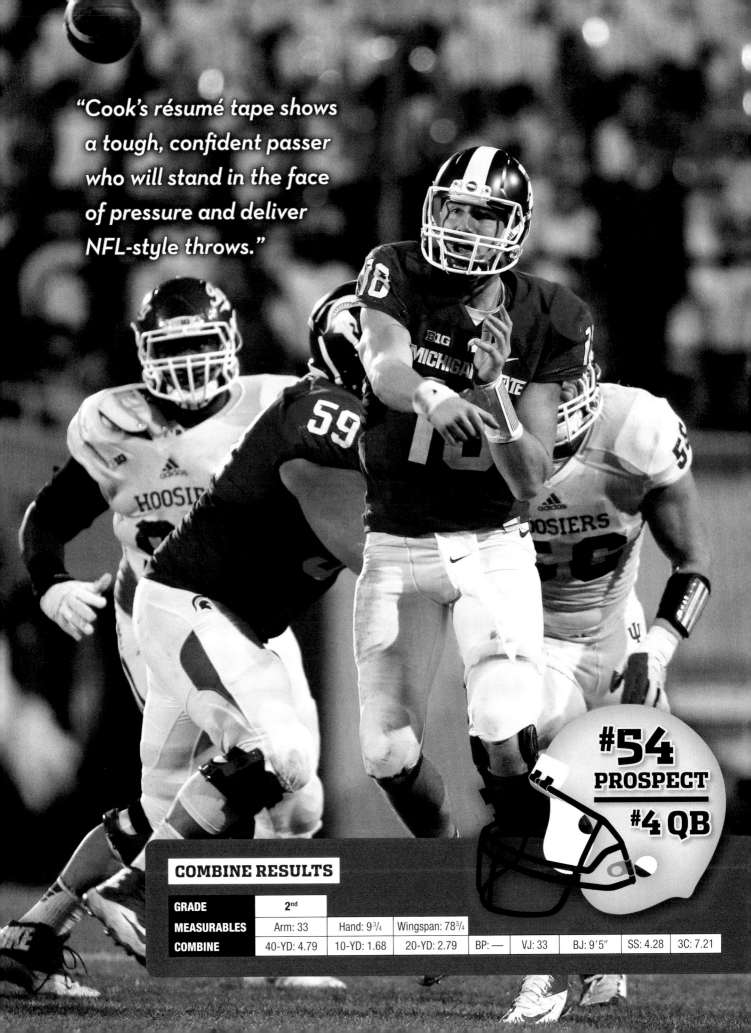

"Cook's résumé tape shows a tough, confident passer who will stand in the face of pressure and deliver NFL-style throws."

#54 PROSPECT
#4 QB

COMBINE RESULTS

GRADE	2nd							
MEASURABLES	Arm: 33	Hand: 9¾	Wingspan: 78¾					
COMBINE	40-YD: 4.79	10-YD: 1.68	20-YD: 2.79	BP: —	VJ: 33	BJ: 9'5"	SS: 4.28	3C: 7.21

JASON SPRIGGS
OT / INDIANA

Name: Jason Spriggs

Ht: 6′5⅝″ **Wt:** 301

Hometown/High School: Elkhart, IN / Concord

Class: Senior

Number: 78

DOB: May 17, 1994

Career Highlights: Senior Bowl (2016), Second-Team All-American (2015), Second-Team All–Big Ten (2015), Honorable Mention All–Big Ten (2012)

Did You Know? Was voted the top offensive lineman by NFL scouts during the week of practices at the 2016 Senior Bowl.

Fun Fact: Spriggs was a five-sport athlete in high school, playing soccer, baseball, lacrosse, and track and field along with football as a prep athlete.

Ideal Team Fit: Although not ready to start in the NFL as a rookie, Spriggs' best football is ahead of him with the body control and frame to develop into a swing tackle.

NFL Comparison: Anthony Castonzo

Depending on the school, Jason Spriggs was recruited as a tight end, defensive lineman, and offensive lineman, receiving mostly MAC attention until Indiana entered the picture, offering him a scholarship to play tackle for the Hoosiers. He earned the starting left tackle job as a true freshman in 2012, starting all 12 games and earning an All–Big Ten Honorable Mention. Spriggs again started all 12 games as a sophomore in 2013 but missed a pair of games due to injury as a junior, starting 10 games at left tackle in 2014. He started all 13 games at left tackle as a senior in 2015, earning second-team All-America and second-team All–Big Ten honors.

STRENGTHS: Athletic frame and long arms, extending well to meet rushers and come to balance at the point of attack. Quickly sets up shop and gets into position. Comfortable on his feet and stays balanced in space, showing good knee bend and overall flexibility. Measured footwork and controlled movements to mirror in pass protection. Understands body angles to wall off run lanes. Intelligent with strong understanding of his responsibilities. Quick eyes and prefers to use his hands to jolt and steer bodies in the run game. Room to get stronger and continue to add bulk. Has the desired competitive temperament for a lineman, fighting through the whistle. Team captain with a blue-collar mentality and goal-oriented mind-set. Four-year starter at left tackle (47 career starts).

WEAKNESSES: Questionable core strength and needs to continue and add thickness to his frame. Base power and technique require refinement. Struggles to keep a consistent center of gravity, popping upright and losing his anchor. Inconsistent punch placement and needs to do a better job controlling the point of attack once engaged. Inconsistent bender, causing him to struggle with counters and moving targets. Needs to better drive through his hips as a run blocker, struggling to consistently unleash his power to finish. Will lower his eye level and whiff on cut block attempts.

SUMMARY: A lanky athlete when he arrived in Bloomington, Spriggs weighed only 260 pounds as a senior in high school, but the Hoosiers coaching staff worked hard to develop his skills, and four years later, he is now a legitimate NFL prospect. (Indiana head coach Kevin Wilson on Spriggs: "His skill-set is as talented as any lineman I've coached.") While he has worked hard to fill out his frame, Spriggs plays with a tall center of gravity and his strength limitations allow bull rushers to go right through him. His ability to recover on the move requires attention, but Spriggs has the frame, body control, and awareness needed to develop into an NFL starter, showing a strong understanding of his responsibilities to get the job done.

CAREER STATS

SEASON	GP/GS	POS
2012	12/12	LT
2013	12/12	LT
2014	11/10	LT
2015	13/13	LT
Career	48/47	LT

"Spriggs has the frame, body control, and awareness needed to develop into an NFL starter."

#55 PROSPECT
#6 OT

COMBINE RESULTS

GRADE	2nd							
MEASURABLES	Arm: 34	Hand: 10⅛	Wingspan: 81⅜					
COMBINE	40-YD: 4.94	10-YD: 1.76	20-YD: 2.90	BP: 31	VJ: 31½	BJ: 9'7"	SS: 4.44	3C: 7.70

JOSHUA PERRY
LB / OHIO STATE

Name: Joshua Perry

Ht: 6′3¾″ **Wt:** 254

Hometown/High School: Galena, OH / Olentangy

Class: Senior

Number: 37

DOB: April 26, 1994

Career Highlights: Senior Bowl (2016), First-Team All–Big Ten (2015), CFP National Champion (2015), Second-Team All–Big Ten (2014)

Did You Know? Finished top-five twice in the long jump at the state track and field championships in high school and set a personal-best leap of 23 feet.

Fun Fact: Recognized for his achievements on the field and effort in the community as one of the 22 members of the 2015 All-State "Good Works Team."

Ideal Team Fit: Although he doesn't have playmaking instincts, Perry should play in the NFL for a long time due to his well-rounded skill-set and versatility that will appeal to 3-4 and 4-3 schemes.

NFL Comparison: Karlos Dansby

"Impeccable character, great work ethic, and extremely intelligent." That's how Ohio State head coach Urban Meyer describes Joshua Perry. And he's pretty talented on the field too. After recording 64 tackles as the starting strong-side linebacker in 2013, Perry moved to the weak side as a junior and led the team in tackles (124), adding 8.5 tackles for loss and his only career interception to earn second-team All–Big Ten. He returned for his senior year and again hit triple-digit tackles (105), earning first-team all-conference honors in 2015.

STRENGTHS: Good-sized athlete with a thick trunk, long arms, and sculpted frame. Worked hard to transform and max out his body. Quick first step and long legs to cover a lot of ground. Plays smooth and easily opens his hips to redirect in coverage. Highly intelligent on and off the field, sniffing out screens and diagnosing play speed well. Instinctive in man or zone coverage and comfortable with his back to the ball. Fills hard against the run and arrives with violence. Excellent timing and closing speed and as a blitzer, shooting gaps with power and making it tough for blockers to slow him down. Versatile experience with playing time at all three linebacker spots (27 career starts). Determined competitor and a reliable ambassador for the sport due to his mature character and intangibles—team captain and glue of the Ohio State defense.

WEAKNESSES: Lacks elite top-end speed in pursuit and doesn't play with multiple gears. Aggressive approach takes him out of plays at times and needs to better hold outside contain. Needs to better collect himself on the move to break down and keep a low strike zone. Pad level needs work, playing too leggy and allowing blockers to attack his chest. Needs to do a better job keeping himself clean and improve his shed technique, struggling to anticipate and leverage blocks—doesn't need to prove his physicality at the point of attack. Caught on his heels and needs to stay balanced in his movements.

SUMMARY: A three-year starter in Ohio State's 4-3 scheme, Perry has experience at all three linebacker spots and the Buckeyes coaches added more and more to his plate over the years. He has the size of a defensive end, but moves like a linebacker to be equally productive blitzing, dropping in coverage, or pursuing against the run. Perry already carries himself like a professional, and his work habits and mental makeup will make him a quick favorite in an NFL building. Although not elite in any one area on the field, he is very well-rounded with the scheme-diverse skill-set and intangibles that will make him a fit for all 32 defenses.

CAREER STATS

SEASON	GP/GS	TACKLES	TFL	SACKS	FF	INT
2012	10/0	5	0.0	0.0	0	0
2013	13/10	64	2.0	1.0	0	0
2014	15/14	124	8.5	3.0	1	1
2015	13/13	105	7.5	3.5	0	0
Career	51/37	298	18.0	7.5	1	1

> "Perry already carries himself like a professional, and his work habits and mental makeup will make him a quick favorite in an NFL building."

#56 PROSPECT

#7 LB

COMBINE RESULTS

GRADE	2nd–3rd							
MEASURABLES	Arm: 33⅞	Hand: 10	Wingspan: 81½					
COMBINE	40-YD: 4.68	10-YD: 1.64	20-YD: 2.72	BP: 20	VJ: 33½	BJ: 10′4″	SS: —	3C: —

SHILIQUE CALHOUN
DE / MICHIGAN STATE

Name: Shilique Calhoun

Ht: 6′4⅜″ **Wt:** 251

Hometown/High School: Middletown, NJ / Middletown North

Class: Redshirt Senior

Number: 89

DOB: March 20, 1992

Career Highlights: First-Team All–Big Ten (2015), All-American (2015), First-Team All–Big Ten (2014), All-American (2014), First-Team All–Big Ten (2013), All-American (2013), Smith-Brown Big Ten Defensive Lineman of the Year (2013)

Did You Know? Leaves East Lansing second all-time in sacks (27) and fourth in tackles for loss (44), as over a third of his career tackles came behind the line of scrimmage.

Fun Fact: Grew up playing basketball, but was coaxed to the football field in high school and has come a long way since he was a 215-pound, two-way player as a senior.

Ideal Team Fit: Undersized and explosive edge rusher who has limitations versus the run, but will earn his paychecks threatening quarterbacks, ideally as a wide-nine end in a 4-3 or standing up in a 3-4 scheme.

NFL Comparison: Demarcus Lawrence

One of the most accomplished defenders in Michigan State history, Shilique Calhoun became a starter for the Spartans as a sophomore and earned All-America and All–Big Ten honors each of the last three seasons. He burst onto the scene in 2013 with 14 tackles for loss and 7.5 sacks to earn Big Ten Defensive Lineman of the Year honors. Calhoun had his most productive season as a senior in 2015 with 49 tackles, 15 tackles for loss, and 10.5 sacks.

STRENGTHS: Tall with good length and room to add 10–15 pounds of muscle. Good initial quickness and long strides to beat most college offensive tackles to the corner. Smooth bender with natural flexibility to dip with low pad level and make quick inside moves. Active hands and uses his upper and lower body in unison to shock blockers when he leans to transition momentum to power. Easily changes directions in space with a fluid lower body. Heady and improved recognition to string runs outside and blow up screens. Uses his length to tie up blockers in the run game and has improved his point of attack strength. Closes fast and arrives at the ball carrier with a physical mentality. Elevates well to obstruct passing lanes and make plays on special teams (two career blocked field goals). Three-year starter and durable, starting the last 41 consecutive games. Two-year team captain with a coachable attitude.

WEAKNESSES: High-hipped and long-legged, which forces him to frequently pop upright off the snap. Lean-bone structure and muscle tone. Poor shed technique and too easily hung up on single blocks when initial speed move is ineffective. Offenses can run at him as he struggles to win with power once his momentum is halted. Undeveloped hand use and pass-rush moves are predictable. Bad habit of lowering his head, losing sight of his target and restricting his ball awareness. Will leave production on the field and needs to be a more consistent finisher. Not a glass-eater and has some passive tendencies.

SUMMARY: A three-year starter, Calhoun lined up in a three-point stance at both left and right defensive end for the Spartans' four-man front, occasionally moving inside to three-technique on obvious passing downs. Calhoun is a momentum rusher with the initial quickness, long-striding speed, and natural shoulder dip to capture the corner, but he is too easily slowed at contact and is missing a power element. He isn't a point-of-attack player and allows blockers to knock him off balance, which limits his NFL ceiling as a run defender, but Calhoun has the pass-rush traits to contribute early in his career as a sub-package rusher while pushing for starting snaps.

CAREER STATS

SEASON	GP/GS	TACKLES	TFL	SACKS	FF
2012	13/0	6	2.5	1.0	0
2013	14/14	37	14.0	7.5	2
2014	13/13	39	12.5	8.0	1
2015	14/14	49	15.0	10.5	1
Career	54/41	131	44.0	27.0	4

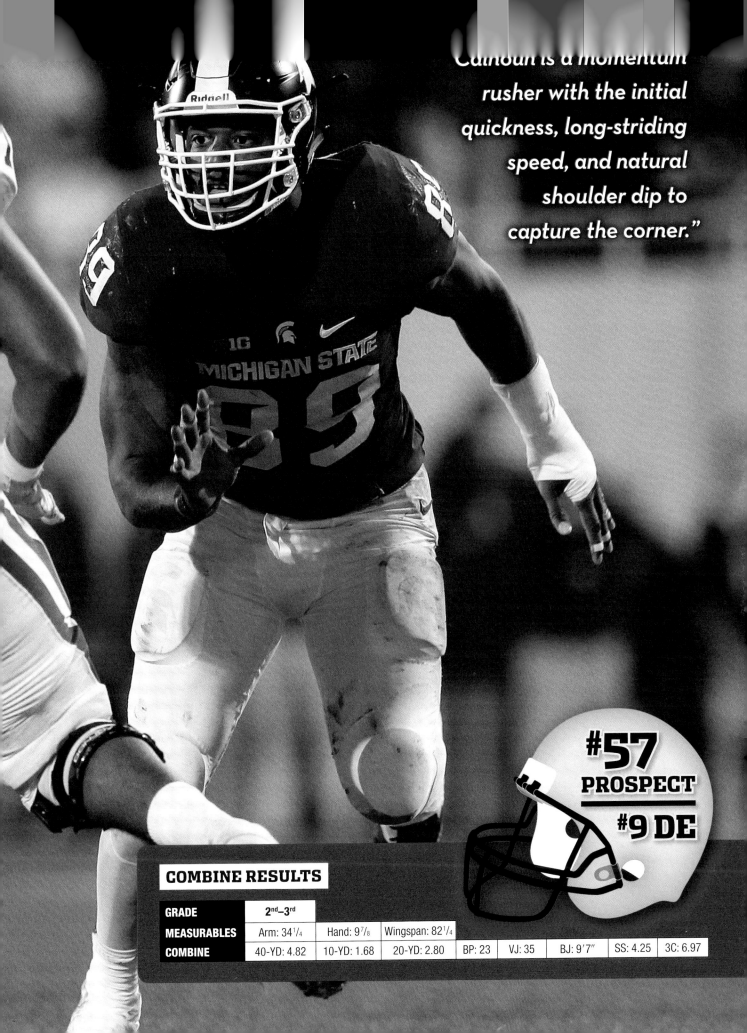

Calhoun is a momentum rusher with the initial quickness, long-striding speed, and natural shoulder dip to capture the corner."

#57 PROSPECT

#9 DE

COMBINE RESULTS

GRADE	2nd–3rd							
MEASURABLES	Arm: 34¼	Hand: 9⅞	Wingspan: 82¼					
COMBINE	40-YD: 4.82	10-YD: 1.68	20-YD: 2.80	BP: 23	VJ: 35	BJ: 9'7"	SS: 4.25	3C: 6.97

KYLER FACKRELL
LB / UTAH STATE

Name: Kyler Fackrell

Ht: 6'5" **Wt:** 245

Hometown/High School: Mesa, AZ / Mesa

Class: Redshirt Senior

Number: 9

DOB: November 25, 1991

Career Highlights: Senior Bowl (2016), First-Team All-MWC (2015), Second-Team All-WAC (2013), First-Team All-WAC (2012), Freshman All-American (2012)

Did You Know? An older prospect (will turn 25 years old during the NFL season), Fackrell and his wife, Elizabeth, have a one-year-old daughter, Delaney.

Fun Fact: Most prospects played multiple sports in high school, but few starred on the volleyball court like Fackrell, who was a two-time letter-winner.

Ideal Team Fit: A light-footed and long-armed athlete, Fackrell offers intriguing versatility, but does his best work in space, fitting best as a starting 3-4 edge rusher who can rush or drop in space.

NFL Comparison: A taller Connor Barwin

A quarterback, wide receiver, linebacker, and safety in high school, Kyler Fackrell was widely under-recruited and didn't receive any FBS-level scholarships until Utah State (his father's alma mater) offered late in the process. After redshirting in 2011, he became a starter and garnered Freshman All-America honors with 87 tackles, including eight for loss. He started all 14 games as a sophomore in 2013 and again earned all-conference honors, but missed almost all of the next season due to a knee injury in the opener. Fackrell returned healthy in 2015 as a senior and led the team with 15 tackles for loss, adding 82 tackles and four sacks to earn first-team All–Mountain West honors.

STRENGTHS: Tall, long-levered frame. Worked hard to develop his muscle and limb strength (only 200 pounds when he arrived at Utah State). Loose athlete with smooth redirection skills and long strides to cover a lot of ground. Lateral quickness to sidestep blocks or string plays to the outside. Active rusher and quick to read, adjust his angle, and close—blockers don't have an answer for his stunts or loops in space. Uses his length to engage and lock out. Looks natural in reverse and has experience in coverage. Offers athletic versatility and natural ball skills (eight passes defended and four interceptions in his career). Played on special teams coverages in college, including one blocked kick. Accountable and hard-working, but also feisty and competitive. Football junkie and singled out as the leader of the defense by his head coach.

WEAKNESSES: Lean-muscled body type with lanky bulk. Not a forceful player at the point of attack and needs to develop his take-on strength to push through the shoulder of blockers. Plays tall and too easily caught up in the crowd. Quick hands, but shed technique and block recognition requires fine-tuning. Needs to better break down and finish in space. Long-legged mover, leading to choppy steps and lost balance in short-areas. Inconsistent backfield vision and anticipation, which leads to overaggressive tendencies. Missed all of the 2014 season due to an ACL tear in his right knee (August 2014).

SUMMARY: A three-year starter, Fackrell lined up as an edge rusher and outside linebacker in Utah State's 3-4 base, playing a jack-of-all-trades role as a rusher and cover man. He is tall, long, and flexible with athletic range and closing burst, doing his best work in space—has the ball skills to be a legitimate tight end prospect. Fackrell isn't a power player and can be too easily controlled at the point of attack, but the competitive toughness is there. NFL scouts like his athleticism, intangibles, and effort, but it's his role versatility that will get him drafted early in the 2016 NFL Draft.

CAREER STATS

SEASON	GP/GS	TACKLES	TFL	SACKS	FF	INT
2012	13/13	87	8.0	3.0	1	3
2013	14/14	82	13.0	5.0	2	1
2014	1/1	2	0.0	0.0	0	0
2015	13/13	82	15.0	4.0	2	0
Career	41/41	253	36.0	12.0	5	4

"NFL scouts like his athleticism, intangibles, and effort, but it's his role versatility that will get him drafted early."

#58 PROSPECT
#8 LB

COMBINE RESULTS

GRADE	2nd–3rd							
MEASURABLES	Arm: 33	Hand: 10 1/8	Wingspan: 80					
COMBINE	40-YD: 4.72	10-YD: 1.61	20-YD: 2.75	BP: 15	VJ: 34 1/2	BJ: 10'1"	SS: —	3C: —

KENTRELL BROTHERS
LB / MISSOURI

Name: Kentrell Brothers

Ht: 6'⅜" **Wt:** 245

Hometown/High School: Guthrie, OK / Guthrie

Class: Redshirt Senior

Number: 10

DOB: February 8, 1993

Career Highlights: Senior Bowl (2016), First-Team All-SEC (2015), All-American (2015)

Did You Know? Highly productive starting experience with 120-plus tackles each of the last two years, leading the country in tackles per game (12.7) as a senior.

Fun Fact: Wears the No. 72 on his wrist tape to honor the high school jersey number of his friend Tyler Nichols, who passed away.

Ideal Team Fit: A player whose tackling abilities will trump scheme, Brothers projects best inside in a 3-4 scheme like the New Orleans Saints or strong-side in a 4-3 base like the Atlanta Falcons.

NFL Comparison: D'Qwell Jackson

Overlooked by in-state programs like Oklahoma and Oklahoma State out of high school, Kentrell Brothers committed to Missouri, the first school who offered him. After redshirting due to injury and serving as a backup in 2012, he earned the starting weak-side linebacker role as a sophomore in 2013 (14 starts), recording 70 tackles and three interceptions. He started all 14 games again in 2014 as a junior, leading the team with 122 tackles and three forced fumbles. Brothers had his most productive season as a senior in 2015 with a SEC-best 152 tackles, leading the team with 12 tackles for loss to earn first-team All-SEC and All-America honors.

STRENGTHS: Looks good on the hoof with proportionate body thickness. Processes action quickly with above-average instincts for the position. Smart pre-snap, recognizing formations and anticipating play calls. Reliable play speed and quick to work through the trash. Excellent at coming to balance on the move and breaking down to be a dependable open-field tackler. Finds that balance between patience, aggressiveness, and staying alert. Physical player who uses his aggressive hands to stack-and-shed. Lateral agility as a blitzer. Impact player on special teams coverages (three blocked kicks in 2015). Excellent timing with a knack for the big play with 16 passes defended, five interceptions, and four forced fumbles over his career. Durable and tough, playing through pain—started 40 straight games the last three seasons.

WEAKNESSES: Lacks ideal height and arm length (under 31 inches), requiring help at times to finish tackles. Not an explosive mover with only one gear in pursuit, limiting his chase speed and overall range. Lacks the secondary burst to recover after a false step. Overaggressive tendencies, biting on fakes and abandoning his cover responsibilities. Heavy feet and tight joints show up in coverage, struggling to cover one-on-one consistently in man. Needs to be a more reliable finisher in small spaces like the pocket. Lack of ideal size and athletic traits makes his margin for error miniscule.

SUMMARY: A three-year starter in Missouri's 4-3 base scheme, Brothers played primarily weak-side linebacker, moving to the middle in nickel situations. He is a high-volume tackler with more stops the last two seasons than any other college football player, registering double-digit tackles in 11 of 12 games in 2015. Brothers plays with above-average recognition skills and anticipation to beat blockers to the contact point, but for his high tackle production, he also misses several tackles due to his lack of ideal speed and length. However, he's able to compensate for his average athleticism due to his competitive instincts to be a ball magnet and tackling machine.

CAREER STATS

SEASON	GP/GS	TACKLES	TFL	SACKS	FF	INT
2012	11/0	14	0.0	0.0	0	0
2013	14/14	70	6.5	1.0	0	3
2014	14/14	122	5.0	1.0	3	0
2015	12/12	152	12.0	2.5	1	2
Career	51/40	358	23.5	4.5	4	5

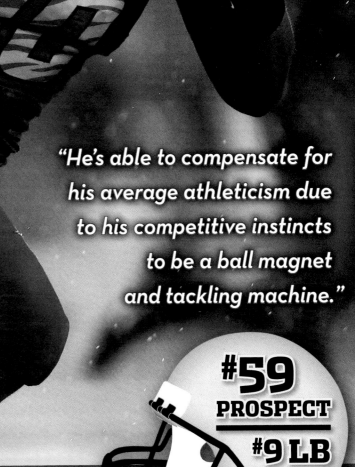

"He's able to compensate for his average athleticism due to his competitive instincts to be a ball magnet and tackling machine."

#59 PROSPECT

#9 LB

COMBINE RESULTS

GRADE	2nd–3rd							
MEASURABLES	Arm: 30¾	Hand: 9¾	Wingspan: 76					
COMBINE	40-YD: 4.89	10-YD: 1.68	20-YD: 2.84	BP: 19	VJ: 28½	BJ: 9'2"	SS: 4.11	3C: 6.99

CHRISTIAN HACKENBERG
QB / PENN STATE

Name: Christian Hackenberg

Ht: 6′4⅜″ **Wt:** 223

Hometown/High School: Palmyra, VA / Fork Union

Class: Junior

Number: 14

DOB: February 14, 1995

Career Highlights: Thompson–Randel El Big Ten Freshman of the Year (2013), Freshman All-American (2013)

Did You Know? Leaves Penn State with school records for career passing yards (8,457), completions (693), and 300-yard passing games (nine).

Fun Fact: Not only did he stay committed to Penn State after the program was hit with sanctions by the NCAA, but Hackenberg worked hard to keep the Nittany Lions' 2013 recruiting class together.

Ideal Team Fit: Reuniting with Bill O'Brien in Houston makes obvious sense, but Hackenberg needs to land where he won't be expected to see the field for at least one full season and can learn behind a seasoned veteran. The Arizona Cardinals would be a great fit.

NFL Comparison: Mix of Jay Cutler and Logan Thomas

A quarterback prospect who fits the mold of what NFL teams covet at the position, Christian Hackenberg had a roller-coaster career at Penn State, and that turbulence will likely continue through the draft. Under the tutelage of Bill O'Brien, he earned Big Ten Freshman of the Year honors in 2013, but following O'Brien's departure to the NFL, Hackenberg's development was stunted the past two seasons under the new coaching staff. He set career lows as a junior in 2015 with a 53.5% completion rate and 2,525 passing yards, though he did improve his touchdown-to-interception ratio (16/6).

STRENGTHS: Ideal physical build and height for the position. Loose and live arm to rip lasers with above-average zip. Effortless deep-ball thrower. Toughness isn't a question with the size to take consistent punishment and bounce back. Quick-footed athlete for his size with clean footwork in his three-, five-, and seven-step drops. Two-year team captain (second youngest player to be elected captain in school history) and viewed as a leader in the locker room. Well-respected on campus, especially for the way he handled adversity after Penn State was punished with NCAA sanctions.

WEAKNESSES: Marginal awareness in the pocket, struggles to navigate around the noise. Slow to process due to questionable vision. Immature eye use, staring down targets and predetermining throws, which leads to inexplicable decisions. Wasn't consistently asked to work sideline-to-sideline in his progressions. Confidence needs to be rebuilt. Too relaxed and needs to show more urgency from snap to release. Highly inconsistent ball placement and downfield touch, struggling to control his ball speeds. Upper- and lower-half mechanics are often on different pages, affecting his accuracy (completion percentage dropped each season). Deer in headlights when blitzed. Played behind a shaky O-line (sacked 103 times in his career), but too many of those hits were of his own doing, holding the ball too long and clamming up under pressure.

SUMMARY: A three-year starter, Hackenberg had a promising freshman season with O'Brien and wide receiver Allen Robinson, but he regressed the last two seasons without them. He didn't receive much help with questionable play-calling, inconsistent weapons, and a leaky line, but Hackenberg deserves plenty of blame. He has special arm talent and is able to make throws other QBs are unable to make. But he doesn't show a natural feel for the game and lacks a strong grasp in critical areas of the position: touch, placement, and decision-making. No doubt Hackenberg will benefit from NFL coaching, but the game still moves at light speed for him and hasn't shown signs of slowing down. Although the tape shows a mid- to late-round project, Hackenberg has the physical traits and arm strength that will convince an NFL team he is worth the risk in the first two rounds.

CAREER STATS

SEASON	GP/GS	CMP	ATT	PCT	YDS	TDS	INT
2013	12/12	231	392	58.9	2,955	20	10
2014	13/13	270	484	55.8	2,977	12	15
2015	13/13	192	359	53.5	2,525	16	6
Career	38/38	693	1,235	56.1	8,457	48	31

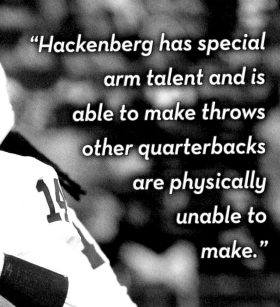

"Hackenberg has special arm talent and is able to make throws other quarterbacks are physically unable to make."

#60 PROSPECT

#5 QB

COMBINE RESULTS

GRADE	2ⁿᵈ–3ʳᵈ							
MEASURABLES	Arm: 32	Hand: 9	Wingspan: 77³/₄					
COMBINE	40-YD: 4.78	10-YD: 1.64	20-YD: 2.82	BP: —	VJ: 31	BJ: 9'6"	SS: 4.33	3C: 7.04

THE NEXT 60 (PROSPECTS 61–120)

Rk.	Player	Pos.	School	Rk.	Player	Pos.	School
61.	Xavien Howard	CB	Baylor	91.	Karl Joseph	S	West Virginia
62.	Sterling Shepard	WR	Oklahoma	92.	Thomas Duarte	TE	UCLA
63.	Ronald Blair	DE	Appalachian State	93.	Rashard Robinson	CB	LSU
64.	Sheldon Day	DT	Notre Dame	94.	Joe Dahl	OG	Washington State
65.	Hassan Ridgeway	DT	Texas	95.	Jordan Howard	RB	Indiana
66.	Jihad Ward	DE	Illinois	96.	Jonathan Williams	RB	Arkansas
67.	Devontae Booker	RB	Utah	97.	Charles Tapper	DE	Oklahoma
68.	Kenny Lawler	WR	California	98.	Keanu Neal	S	Florida
69.	Adolphus Washington	DT	Ohio State	99.	Alex Collins	RB	Arkansas
70.	Nick Martin	C	Notre Dame	100.	Jerald Hawkins	OT	LSU
71.	Kenneth Dixon	RB	Louisiana Tech	101.	Leonte Carroo	WR	Rutgers
72.	Jalen Mills	CB	LSU	102.	Denver Kirkland	OG	Arkansas
73.	Chris Jones	DT	Mississippi State	103.	Christian Westerman	OG	Arizona State
74.	Will Redmond	CB	Mississippi State	104.	Joe Schobert	LB	Wisconsin
75.	Carl Nassib	DE	Penn State	105.	Kolby Listenbee	WR	TCU
76.	Darian Thompson	S	Boise State	106.	Dak Prescott	QB	Mississippi State
77.	Harlan Miller	CB	S.E. Louisiana	107.	Miles Killebrew	S	Southern Utah
78.	Maliek Collins	DT	Nebraska	108.	Bronson Kaufusi	DE	BYU
79.	Javon Hargrave	DT	South Carolina State	109.	Paul Perkins	RB	UCLA
80.	Germain Ifedi	OT	Texas A&M	110.	Cardale Jones	QB	Ohio State
81.	Antonio Morrison	LB	Florida	111.	Maurice Canady	CB	Virginia
82.	C.J. Prosise	RB	Notre Dame	112.	Darius Latham	DT	Indiana
83.	Deion Jones	LB	LSU	113.	Matt Ioannidis	DT	Temple
84.	Scooby Wright	LB	Arizona	114.	Vadal Alexander	OG	LSU
85.	Joshua Garnett	OG	Stanford	115.	Shawn Oakman	DE	Baylor
86.	Roberto Aguayo	K	Florida State	116.	Cyrus Jones	CB	Alabama
87.	D.J. Reader	DT	Clemson	117.	Austin Hooper	TE	Stanford
88.	Jordan Jenkins	LB	Georgia	118.	Rees Odhiambo	OG	Boise State
89.	Nick Vannett	TE	Ohio State	119.	Kelvin Taylor	RB	Florida
90.	Le'Raven Clark	OT	Texas Tech	120.	Tyler Higbee	TE	Western Kentucky